The
BEST of
Reader's
Digest

Reader's
Digest
New York / Montreal

Chief Content Officer,
Reader's Digest Jason Buhrmester
Content Director Mark Hagen
Creative Director Raeann Thompson
Senior Editor Julie Kuczynski
Editor Christine Campbell
Associate Creative Director
Kristen Stecklein
Assistant Art Director
Samantha Primuth
Deputy Editor, Copy Desk
Ann M. Walter
Copy Editor Suchismita Ukil

A READER'S DIGEST BOOK

Copyright © 2024 Trusted
Media Brands, Inc.
485 Lexington Avenue
New York, NY 10017

The credits that appear on pages
286-288 are hereby made part of this
copyright page.

ISBN 979-8-88977-029-9
(retail hardcover)
ISBN 979-8-88977-028-2
(dated hardcover)
ISBN 979-8-88977-046-6
(undated hardcover)

Component numbers
116600119H (dated)
116600121H (undated)

We are committed to both the quality
of our products and the service we
provide to our customers. We value
your comments, so please feel free
to contact us at *TMBBookTeam@
TrustedMediaBrands.com*.

For more *Reader's Digest* products
and information, visit our website:
www.rd.com (in the United States)
www.readersdigest.ca (in Canada)

Printed in China
10 9 8 7 6 5 4 3 2 1

Text, photography and illustrations
for *The Best of Reader's Digest* are based
on articles previously published in
Reader's Digest magazine (*rd.com*).

CONTENTS

INTRODUCTION

For over a century, *Reader's Digest* has been a platform for gripping narratives that truly span the spectrum of the human experience. With everything from daring rescues and inspiring biographies to heartwarming tales and hilarious takes on modern life, this collection includes some of the most thrilling, touching and humorous articles from our archives.

In this compilation we included "—And Sudden Death." A blockbuster for *Reader's Digest* in 1935, this incredible piece was one of the most widely read articles of its time. Also found here is the magazine's first in a popular series called "The Most Unforgettable Character I Ever Met." The story, "The Doctor of Lennox," tells of a man's pioneering courage while charting his own course—despite situations others deemed as obstacles. In addition, a profound account of a young Egyptian girl being held against her will acts as testament to what the spirit can endure.

Alongside these and many other favorites, we've curated sensational photographs, uproarious jokes, playful cartoons, insightful quotes and true stories from readers like you. Plus, enjoy bonus material never before published in the magazine.

So buckle up for a journey through the extraordinary, heart-wrenching and downright delightful—happy reading!

—The Editors of *Reader's Digest*

Trapped!

by Lee Karsian, as told to Albert Rosenfeld

The water rose to his knees, his waist, his armpits—a young sailor's terrible 20 hours in a sinking ship

It was D-Day in the Philippines—October 20, 1944. American troops were already three miles inland on the island of Leyte when, shortly after 4 p.m., a Japanese plane emerged from the mists and loosed a torpedo at the cruiser *Honolulu*. The explosion tore a jagged 25-foot hole in the ship's port side, killing 60 men.

As the ship sagged over, the sea flooded the third deck and part of the second. But down on the third deck there remained one lone pocket of air: the compartment known as Radio 3. And trapped inside Radio 3 was Lee Karsian, a 19-year-old radioman third class.

Around noon, hot and tired, I had wandered into Radio 3, our emergency radio shack. It was a small room, about 8 by 12 feet, but the fan in there felt wonderful. I dogged down the hatch, spread out a blanket, took off my shoes and went contentedly to sleep.

When I awoke, my watch said 4:05—already five minutes late for duty. I scrambled to my feet and stooped over to get my shoes. Before I could straighten up again I felt myself weirdly lifted, then slammed face down onto the steel deck. In the same instant the lights went out, there was a lightning-quick flash of flame and a slow-building explosive roar. Things landed heavily on my back; a thick dust filled the air. I heard water rushing against the hatch, blood-freezing screams from outside—and then I blacked out.

I have no idea how much time passed before I came to. Smoke and dust filled my nostrils, and there was a foul taste in my mouth. I ached all over. The floor was wet under me. With great effort, I slid two metal transmitter plates off my back. Then in the darkness I staggered around the tilted deck.

Things looked bad. Water was coming in fast. The radio was dead. So was the battery on the battle light. I took a heavy file from the workbench and banged on the bulkheads. No response. Sloshing around in the watery dark, I finally found a saucer-sized shrapnel hole, with water pouring in. I knew I was trapped, but I felt better after I had stuffed the hole with the innards of a mattress I found under the workbench. When I found a flashlight that worked, I felt even better—but not for long. The roving light revealed thousands of tiny holes the size of pinheads, through which oily water was seeping steadily. Panic began seeping into my pores.

Seized with a violent coughing fit, I leaned weakly against the workbench for support. My flashlight went out, plunging me into blackness again. Now panic took a firmer grip. I felt like crying, I *wanted* to cry—but I couldn't.

Suddenly I remembered the battle phones that connected with the ship's intercom. I waded over and frantically plugged them in, holding the earphones to my ears.

"… Signals Aft testing with Signal Bridge." It was a familiar voice.

"John!" I said, surprised at the steadiness of my voice. "John, this is Lee Karsian."

"Lee Karsian? You're dead!" Then, "Where are you?"

"I'm trapped in Radio 3."

Everyone began cutting in on the line. A voice came in from the main deck. "This is Captain Thurber. Can you hear me? We'll do everything in our power to get you out as soon as possible." Then I heard Bill Gallagher, my closest buddy. "Bill," I said, "I want the truth. Are we sinking?"

He hesitated. "Lee, they're lightening ship, trying to keep her afloat if they possibly can. If there's anything more, I'll let you know. I won't leave these phones for a minute."

Another coughing fit caught me in the pit of my stomach, and I passed out. But as my face hit the water, which was now over my knees, the shock revived me. I leaned shakily against the bulkhead, lost all track of time.

Suddenly, "Karsian, can you hear me?" It was one of our officers.

"I'm sorry to have to tell you this, but it looks as if we're going to abandon ship. It's not official yet, but as soon as it is, one of our destroyers will be given the order to sink the ship. We'll ask them to make the hit as direct as possible."

The voice cut out, and Bill came back on. "Lee! Do you have anything to knock yourself out with?"

I had already checked. The medicine kit contained a strip of easy-to-jab morphine ampoules. "If I go down," I said, "I'll go down sleeping."

"Okay. I'll be the last guy off. When I go, you'll know it's time to use it." We both seemed terribly businesslike.

The next voice was Chaplain Sharkey's. The day before I had told him, jokingly, that I had tickets for the Army-Navy football game. "I guess I won't get to use those tickets after all," I said feebly.

"No, I guess not," the chaplain said.

I passed out again, then gradually became aware of the chaplain's voice: "… walk through the valley of the shadow of death, I will fear no evil, for Thou art with me. Thy rod and Thy staff, they comfort me …" I did feel comforted. Then, with a sickening jolt, I realized what the chaplain was doing. *He was reading my funeral service!*

His voice droned on, but my mind strayed. I thought of my home in Union City, New Jersey. I could see my father listening to the radio, my mother finishing the dishes in the kitchen. Suddenly the chaplain's voice stopped.

"Bill!" I called in panic. "Bill!"

"Yes, Lee. Listen—it looks like we have a reprieve. There's a destroyer standing by, and two tugs are on the port side holding us up. They're going to try to save you—and that means saving the ship."

Another voice, unfamiliar, came in: "We've checked the deck above you, and it's under only about four and a half feet of water. We've sent word to the supply ship to build a cofferdam. We'll put it on your overhead, pump the water out and cut through."

It was a long time before I got any more news. Meanwhile the oily water had risen to my waist, and the coughing was making me steadily thirstier, weaker, sicker. I must have passed out again, for when I came to I noticed that the ship was now on an almost even keel. My elation was short-lived, though.

"I'm sorry, Lee," came Bill's voice. "The cofferdam didn't work. There was no way to get through the overhead without drowning you."

"I was afraid of that."

Now despair overwhelmed me. But after a few minutes Bill came back on again. "Lee, they've found a way to pump out the little fireroom next to Radio 3. They think they can cut through to you from there."

I waited by the bulkhead, listening for sounds of the rescue squad. Bill helped pass the time by talking—about the good times we'd had, about our plans to go into business together. But a lot of time was going by. "What's taking them so long?" I asked angrily. "They can't *do* it, can they?"

"Take it easy," Bill said patiently. "They're in there. Put your hand against the bulkhead."

I moved my hand along the metal. Finally I felt a spot at about eye level that was getting warm. Gradually it grew pink, then red. Seconds later the red-hot spot became a cascade of sparks. They were through!

Suddenly the whole room blazed up in a blinding flash. The sparks had ignited the oil on the water! I screamed for them to stop. Ducking under the water, I fished up my blanket and threw it in front of me. It smothered the flames.

Again I wanted to cry. I stood there panting, up to my armpits in water, knowing I couldn't go on. I was spent, scorched inside and out. My head was light, and I felt that I was going to pass out again. Only this time I wouldn't get up.

"Hey, fella!" someone shouted from the other side of the bulkhead. "We got a hole big as a cigarette now. You want some water?" In a minute a tube was passed through, and I was drinking my fill.

"I feel great now," I announced. "Let's get to work."

The bulkhead was four inches thick, but the cutting job went fairly fast. At last the rescue squad pronounced the hole finished. It didn't look big enough, but it was now or never.

I looked at the sharp, jagged edges, took a deep breath, put my hands over my head and squeezed my shoulders carefully into the hole. Gently, the rescuers started dragging me through. As the steel cut into me, they stopped hauling for a moment. But as I saw the first human faces I had seen in 20 hours I forgot all about the pain. "Pull!" I begged. They did.

When I appeared on deck, black from head to foot with soot and oil, a cheer went up from the sailors. I was taken to sick bay, where there were men wrapped like mummies in thick bandages with the blood soaking through. Chaplain Sharkey left them and came over to me. "They're glad you made it, Lee," said the chaplain. "They were worried about you."

"But they look like they're dying."

"They are."

I sat in silence while my cuts were dressed and the oil was cleaned off. Then I left sick bay and walked along the deck, which was full of dead and wounded. I glanced over at the supply ship, the destroyers, the tugs— I had no idea how many men or how many ships out there in the misty harbor had postponed the war long enough to come to my rescue. Someone brushed into me, rushing toward sick bay. I looked up. It was Bill.

"Lee!" he said, slipping a big arm around my shoulders. "Lee— you're crying."

Originally published in November 1958 issue of *Reader's Digest* magazine.

The Day We Flew the Kites

by Frances Fowler, condensed from *Parents'* magazine

A *childhood experience carries magic through the years*

"STRING!" shouted Brother, bursting into the kitchen. "We need lots more string."

It was Saturday. As always, it was a busy one, for "Six days shalt thou labor and do all thy work" was taken seriously then.

Outside, Father and Mr. Patrick next door were doing chores. Inside the two houses, Mother and Mrs. Patrick were engaged in spring cleaning. Such a windy March day was ideal for "turning out" clothes closets. Already woolens flapped on backyard clotheslines.

Somehow the boys had slipped away to the back lot with their kites. Now even at the risk of having Brother impounded to beat carpets, they had sent him for more string. Apparently there was no limit to the heights to which kites would soar today.

My mother looked out the window. The sky was piercingly blue, the breeze fresh and exciting. Up in all that blueness sailed great puffy billows of clouds. It had been a long, hard winter, but today was spring. Mother looked at the sitting room, its furniture disordered for a Spartan sweeping. Again her eyes wavered toward the window. "Come on, girls!

Let's take string to the boys and watch them fly the kites a minute."

On the way we met Mrs. Patrick, laughing guiltily, escorted by her girls.

There never was such a day for flying kites! God doesn't make two such days in a century. We played all our fresh twine into the boys' kites and still they soared. We could hardly distinguish the tiny, orange-colored specks. Now and then we slowly reeled one in, finally bringing it dipping and tugging to earth, for the sheer joy of sending it up again. What a thrill to run with them, to the right, to the left, and see our poor, earth-bound movements reflected minutes later in their majestic sky dance! We wrote wishes on pieces of paper and slipped them over the string. Slowly, irresistibly, they climbed up until they reached the kites. Surely all such wishes would be granted!

Even our fathers dropped hoe and hammer and joined us. Our mothers took their turns, laughing like schoolgirls. Their hair blew out of their pompadours and curled loose about their cheeks; their gingham aprons whipped about their legs. Mingled with our fun was something akin to awe. The grownups were really playing with us! Once I looked at Mother and thought she was actually pretty. And her over 40!

We never knew where the hours went on that day. There were no hours, just a golden, breezy *now*. I think we were all a little beyond ourselves. Parents forgot their duty and their dignity; children forgot their combativeness and small spites. "Perhaps it's like this in the Kingdom of Heaven," I thought confusedly.

It was growing dark before, drunk with sun and air, we all stumbled sleepily back to the houses. I suppose we had some sort of supper. I suppose there must have been a surface tidying up, for the house on Sunday looked decorous enough.

The strange thing was, we didn't mention that day afterward. I felt a little embarrassed. Surely none of the others had thrilled to it as deeply as I had. I locked the memory up in that deepest part of me where we keep the "things that cannot be and yet are."

The years went on; then one day I was scurrying about my own kitchen in a city apartment, trying to get some work out of the way while my 3-year-old insistently cried her desire to "go park and see ducks."

The Day We Flew the Kites

"I *can't* go!" I said. "I have this and this to do, and when I'm through I'll be too tired to walk that far."

My mother, who was visiting us, looked up from the peas she was shelling. "It's a wonderful day," she offered, "really warm, yet there's a fine, fresh breeze. It reminds me of that day we flew the kites."

I stopped in my dash between stove and sink. The locked door flew open, and with it a gush of memories. I pulled off my apron. "Come on," I told my little girl. "It's too good a day to miss."

Another decade passed. We were in the aftermath of a great war. All evening we had been asking our returned soldier, the youngest Patrick boy, about his experiences as a prisoner of war. He had talked freely, but now for a long time he had been silent. What was he thinking of—what dark and dreadful things?

"Say!" A smile twitched his lips. "Do you remember … no, of course you wouldn't. It probably didn't make the impression on you it did on me."

I hardly dared speak. "Remember what?"

"I used to think of that day a lot in PW camp, when things weren't too good. Do you remember the day we flew the kites?"

Winter came, and the sad duty of a call of condolence on Mrs. Patrick, recently widowed. I dreaded the call. I couldn't imagine how Mrs. Patrick would face life alone.

We talked a little of my family and her grandchildren and the changes in the town. Then she was silent, looking down at her lap. I cleared my throat. Now I must say something about her loss, and she would begin to cry.

When Mrs. Patrick looked up, she was smiling. "I was just sitting here thinking," she said. "Henry had such fun that day. Frances, do you remember the day we flew the kites?"

Originally published in July 1949 issue of *Reader's Digest* magazine.

Humor Hall of Fame

One day a co-worker noticed I had on a new dress. She raved about how beautiful it was and wanted to know where I bought it. I told her the name of the store and jokingly added that if she ended up buying the same dress, she'd have to tell me when she was going to wear it so we didn't show up at the office looking like twins. She replied, "Oh, I'd never wear a dress like that to work!"

—NANCY J. HIMBER

As an amusement park employee, I am often asked for directions to specific attractions. Although detailed maps are given to each customer who enters the park, some people need more help. One exasperated guest approached me after she'd gotten lost using the map. "How come these maps don't have an arrow telling you where you are?" she asked.

—J.B. HAIGHT

Retirement is the best thing that has happened to my brother-in-law. "I never know what day of the week it is," he gloated. "All I know is, the day the big paper comes, I have to dress up and go to church."

—DONALD REICHERT

"This is gobbledygook. I asked for mumbo jumbo."

How Honest Are We?

by Ralph Kinney Bennett

Would you return a wallet filled with money? Reader's Digest *editors set up a test in cities from coast to coast to see what Americans would do.*

It was late afternoon in Greensboro, North Carolina, when Shannon Hill, 28, stopped off at the local IRS office to get tax information for a student-aid application. She was working three jobs, yet barely making ends meet after paying tuition for her classes in radiology. As she was about to walk into the office, she saw a black wallet on the sidewalk.

Inside was $50 in cash—three tens and a 20. *I could sure use this*, she thought. Then she noticed an ID card and a picture of a smiling baby in the wallet. *I'd sure want my money back*, she thought. She called the next day to return the wallet.

Entering the BiLo supermarket in Meadville, Pennsylvania, late one morning, a wiry man in his 30s spotted a tan wallet on a bench. Flipping it open, he fingered the $50 inside, grinned at his companion, a thin woman with brown hair, and stuffed the cash into a pocket of his denim cutoffs. The man turned in the empty wallet at the customer service desk, then left. He and the woman walked rapidly to The Dog Pound bar and went inside, laughing at their sudden fortune.

The wallets these people found were among those a team of *Reader's*

Digest editors "lost" all over America. In each we put a name, local address and phone number, family pictures, notes, coupons—and $50 in cash.

We dropped 120 wallets—10 each in three large cities, three major suburban areas, three medium-sized cities and three small towns. We left them in parking lots, shopping malls, restaurants, gas stations, office buildings and on sidewalks. Then we watched to see what would happen. To each person who returned a wallet, we offered the $50 as a reward.

This was no rigorous scientific study, but rather a real-life test of integrity. Would people in small towns return the wallets more often than those in big cities? Old folks more than young? Women more than men? Every wallet told a story like the ones above—whether of outright theft, a struggle with temptation or a refreshing affirmation of honesty. Here is what we found on our lost-wallet odyssey.

* * *

Seattle bristles with coffee shops, fresh breezes and, in our experience, people eager to do the right thing. Nine of the 10 wallets were returned with the cash inside.

Our most poignant encounter was with a little girl in a pink floral dress. She plucked our wallet off a bench at the amusement park adjacent to the Space Needle and ran to her father. Yong Cha saw a chance to teach his daughter a valuable lesson. He handed the wallet back. "You must take this to the police or someone who can help find the owner," he told her. Mary, age nine, nodded gravely and took her dad's hand as they searched for the park office. "Honesty is the most important thing a child can learn," Cha told us.

Our only disappointment was a stocky, brown-haired man wearing a green shirt with black pin stripes. He found the wallet on a staircase of Seattle's teeming Pike Place market. Examining the cash, he slipped the wallet into a black fanny pack and continued shopping. We never heard from him.

In St. Louis, Philip Taylor found our billfold beside an escalator in the Famous-Barr department store. He left it at the store's customer service office.

Why? Taylor, an investigator for the city's Civil Rights Enforcement Agency, told us, "I'm a Christian, and though I have financial concerns, I have a higher authority to account to." He added that

BIG CITIES

	RETURNED	KEPT
Seattle	9	1
St. Louis	7	3
Atlanta	5	5

he'd twice lost a wallet himself, and remembered how grateful he was when it was returned intact.

In midtown Atlanta, Betty Clark, 50, of East Point, Georgia, found our wallet in the food court of a busy office/shopping complex. Before calling us, she considered turning it over to security but thought "maybe somebody would take the money out of it"—an interesting observation, because Betty is a security supervisor at the nearby High Museum of Art.

She told us a revealing story. Like Yong Cha, Betty's parents had taught her about honesty. But it was a while before the lesson took. "You see, I found a purse one time. I returned it, but I took $20 from it and that $20 bugged me so bad I swore if I ever had the chance again, I'd do the right thing."

But half the Atlantans did the wrong thing. A small, silver-haired woman picked up our wallet at the entrance to a midtown tower, immediately took it into the ground-floor office where she worked, and handed it to the receptionist. Wallet in hand, the receptionist walked through the building's lobby, past the security desk and up the escalator to a restroom. Emerging five minutes later, she came down the escalator and turned the wallet in at the security desk. We immediately recovered it—but the $50 was missing.

*   *   *

Beneath the haze of the Los Angeles basin lies a crescent of suburbs that are incredibly varied in income and culture. Marcella Giannini, slim and stylish in black pants and sleeveless off-white blouse, was among the tourists and afternoon shoppers on Brighton Way in Beverly Hills when she picked up the wallet from the sidewalk.

It never crossed her mind to keep the money. Marcella was "brought up

SUBURBS

	RETURNED	KEPT
Los Angeles	6	4
Houston	5	5
Boston	7	3

Catholic," but now considers herself "more spiritual than religious." Even so, she predicted we would get fewer than half our wallets back because "society's degrading at a fast pace, especially in L.A."

We caught a glimpse of what Marcella meant at the sprawling Del Amo mall south of Los Angeles. Two boys in their early teens happened upon our wallet. One, in shorts and athletic shirt, gave a whoop as he pulled out the money. Talking excitedly, the two walked down the mall, eventually meeting a man who seemed to be the father of one of them. They showed him the wallet. All three left. We never got a call.

"I've had my apartment burglarized to the point where they took every single thing, so welcome to Los Angeles," attorney Istvan Benko told us. He was walking with colleagues to an outdoor lunch when he saw our wallet on a bench in the Century City Shopping Center. He asked people nearby if it was theirs, but no one claimed it. Back at his office, he telephoned us right away.

Near the western suburbs of Houston, Karen McFee, 31, scooped up our billfold outside the West Oaks Mall. She called as soon as she got home. "My own wallet's been stolen a time or two," she explained, "and I thought, well, I wish somebody had returned it."

Outside a discount store on bustling Westheimer Road, a woman in her 60s, wearing a cream-colored pants outfit and pushing a small child in a stroller, picked up our wallet. She examined the contents carefully, then walked to her Cadillac and drove off. We never heard from her.

In Cambridge, Massachusetts, just outside Boston, at the top of the Harvard Square subway escalator, a slim man in his early 20s, wearing black jeans, T-shirt and stereo headphones, picked up the wallet without breaking stride. Slipping it into his pocket, he walked briskly two blocks to an office building. He disappeared into a ground-floor men's room. In a few minutes he came out dressed in the building's security guard uniform and took a seat behind the lobby desk. Later, we called security to ask if a wallet had been returned. It had not.

In nearby Waltham, Massachusetts, a boy with earrings in both ears and a skateboard under his arm noticed our wallet in front of the CVS Pharmacy. In the store, he bought a magazine, then gave the clerk the wallet.

We were about to reward him for returning it, but he shook his head and pulled a $20 bill from his pocket. "I can't take the money," he said. "I was a schmuck and kept this." The boy, who is 18 and works off and on as a landscaper, said he could have used the money to help pay his rent, but "I'm sorry I tried to steal it." He told us, "Morality really messes with you," but added, "that's a good thing."

*　　*　　*

At the corner of Market and Greene streets, near the Jefferson-Pilot complex in Greensboro, North Carolina, a wallet was passed over by many pedestrians until Louis Gentry, an executive with the company, came along. He called the phone number on the ID card—an action he felt was too routine to be worth comment. "Most people are basically honest," he said.

Outside the Belk department store at the Four Seasons mall, however, an elderly woman with a crutch saw one of our wallets. It was all she could do to lean over and pick it up. She examined it several times, then got into a black Buick driven by a man in a dark suit and left. We never heard from them.

In Las Vegas a billfold on the sidewalk outside of the Flamingo Hilton provided a fleeting moral drama. A young man wearing neat blue jeans, a white T-shirt and a silver and gold chain picked up our wallet and looked around at the many passersby. He walked into the Flamingo and seemed to be looking for someone to whom he could give the wallet. He left the Flamingo, entered another casino, eyed the security guards and apparently pondered what to do. Back on the street again, he put the wallet in the front pocket of his jeans and kept walking. After passing several policemen, he disappeared into the crowd and never phoned us.

MEDIUM CITIES

	RETURNED	KEPT
Greensboro, N.C	7	3
Las Vegas	5	5
Dayton, Ohio	5	5

Helen Dubuc, a senior citizen who works at the public library, found our billfold in the Fashion Show Mall on the Vegas Strip. She didn't think people in her city would be much different than elsewhere, although, she told us, "you might get someone who's a little more desperate for money here." In all, five wallets were returned in Las Vegas; five were not.

In Dayton, Ohio, a leathery-faced man in his 60s, wearing a Cincinnati Reds cap and walking with a limp, picked up our wallet outside the Dayton Mall and took it in to the desk at the Hyatt Legal Services office. "Dad worked hard to raise nine of us," Rick Tekulve declared. "He taught us always to pay bills and be honest." Tekulve refused our offer of the $50. "I don't want a reward for doing something I knew was morally right."

On Main Street outside a closed department store, a woman in white slacks, T-shirt and turban-type wrap saw the wallet, doubled back and set her shopping bags around it. She leaned down to fiddle with a pant cuff, then scooped up the wallet and slid it into her bag. She walked over to a bus stop bench, smoked several cigarettes and eventually left. We never heard from her.

In Meadville, Pennsylvania, most people returned our wallets so quickly that our bad impression from the couple who stole the one at the BiLo was eclipsed. Gregory Royds, exhausted from a long day of work as a construction worker, stumbled on a wallet in the Kmart doorway where he was shopping for work boots. The money would have more than paid for the new boots. His girlfriend said, "We've got a name and number here, so we've got to try." They did.

Concord, New Hampshire, provided an interesting take on how people view the honesty of those in neighboring regions. Kimberly Shorrock, 25, a factory worker who turned in a wallet she discovered at the Fort Eddy Mall, said we were lucky to have lost it there rather than in southern New Hampshire because "you've

SMALL TOWNS

	RETURNED	KEPT
Meadville, Pa.	8	2
Concord, N.H.	8	2
Cheyenne, Wyo.	8	2

got the Massachusetts influence down there."

But when Massachusetts resident Steve Rothmel, 34, owner of a pool service company, picked up our wallet outside a Concord restaurant, he called immediately from a cellular phone. He credited his honesty to a "what goes around comes around" philosophy and admitted that seeing a baby picture in the wallet "just hit a spot." (He wasn't the only returner to cite the picture—maybe a baby photo is good insurance for *any* wallet.)

Along Lincoln Way, in the old downtown section of Cheyenne, Wyoming, we left a wallet outside The Wrangler western-wear store. The area gets its share of "drifters and grifters," and we watched as a bowlegged figure in black denims and black T-shirt, with a dark cowboy hat pulled low over his sunglasses, ambled along the sidewalk. He picked up the wallet and proceeded to walk several blocks—until he reached a police station. He turned out to be Jordan Stevenson, a former rodeo rider from Bridger, Montana. "All I could think of was some poor guy without his money," he told us. What made him turn it in? "That's the culture I was raised in."

The bottom line: Out of 120 wallets, 80 were returned—67%. Seattle won the contest for most honest city—nine out of 10 wallets returned intact.

Women outperformed men in our exercise. Of the 60 women who picked up the wallets, 43 returned them with the money still inside—72%. Of the 60 men who picked up the wallets, 37 returned them intact—62%.

Are small towns repositories of virtue? In our case, apart from big city Seattle, apparently so. All three of the smallest cities—Meadville, Concord and Cheyenne—tied for second place, scoring eight out of 10.

Greensboro, St. Louis and the Boston suburbs shared 7-3 records, and the sprawling Los Angeles suburbs–showed six returns and four missing. The poorest record—half returned, half stolen—was shared by Dayton, Atlanta, the Houston suburbs and Las Vegas.

We found some fascinating contrasts between perception and reality. While many of our returners predicted that we would get back fewer than half the wallets, in fact two out of every three were returned intact.

Many returners, both old and young, doubted the honesty of young people. "Youngsters are gonna probably keep it," said Lester Palmer, a former police officer in Meadville. "If they're about 14 to 18, they probably wouldn't return it," declared 21-year-old college student Kim Quails of Lomita, California. "There are kids who will just take the cash and dump the wallet," said Sean Irwin, 18, of Lexington, Massachusetts.

This concern about the morals of youth is long-standing, and it is increasing. In 1938 a Roper poll found that 42% of Americans thought youthful morality was in decline. By 1987 a Yankelovich poll found that general concern had grown to 60% of Americans.

"You don't have to be religious to be honest."

But we might be selling this generation short. Ten of the 15 young people we encountered—from 16-year-old Durango High School junior Alan Kelley at a McDonald's in Las Vegas to 15-year-old Annie Warner of Spokane at a mall stairway near Seattle—returned the wallet and money. Young people tracked right on the 67% average.

This "wallet test" made one thing abundantly clear: our moral compasses are set early by the example of our elders. An overwhelming majority of those who returned the wallets said their desire to do the right thing was instilled by the teaching of parents. Keith Dole, 38, of Greensboro remembered shoplifting as a kid and being taken back to the store by his mother to return the candy, apologize and pay for it. "It taught me a big lesson," he said.

A large number of returners cited their belief in God. And even those who don't regularly attend services often credited religious lessons as a moral prod. But churchgoer Helen Dubuc of Las Vegas said, "You don't have to be religious to be honest."

Priscilla Wilson found a wallet near a slot machine at the Luxor casino in Las Vegas. She quickly distinguished "easy money"—which she hoped to win at the slot machine—from the contents of the wallet on the casino floor. One of 10 children in a poor family, Wilson, along with her brothers and sisters, had been excited when their father—not a particularly religious man—found a cash-filled wallet. "It's somebody else's money," he had admonished them. "We have to return it."

And we were reminded that almost everyone still has a conscience.

How Honest Are We?

All the furtive glances and attempts at concealment we observed from those who intended to keep the money indicated that they knew they were doing wrong.

Whether that sense of right and wrong grows or withers in our society will depend on whether examples of integrity are being set day in, day out. Our experience around the country—from an ex-cowboy in Cheyenne to a factory worker in New Hampshire—suggests that indeed they are.

Originally published in December 1995 issue of *Reader's Digest* magazine.

Nothing in the future exists yet. But anything is possible right now. Including the thing you think you cannot do.

—LAURA MCKOWEN
Author in the book *We Are the Luckiest:*
The Surprising Magic of a Sober Life

WORKING SMARTER, NOT HARDER

I had a co-worker who delighted in finding unpleasant tasks for me, such as sealing a stack of envelopes—for which I used a wet paper towel instead of my tongue. Once, she handed me a long adding machine tape, asking me to find how many items were added together. Instead of counting each item, I used a ruler to figure out items per inch, and then measured the full length of the tape. Our supervisor commended me for handling an unpleasant situation well.

—Mary Garrett, *St. Peters, MO*

THE INVISIBLE CHAUFFEUR

I was getting in the passenger seat and was too lazy to close the car door. I asked my husband, "Who is going to shut the door?" He said "Hold on," stepped on the gas then quickly tapped the brake. The door closed softly by itself. The grandchild thinks it's especially funny.

—Bonnie Raduns, *Basom, NY*

When I Met Caruso

by Elizabeth Bacon Rodewald

A young Quaker girl spends a day in the presence of the famous Italian opera singer, and experiences "extravagance" for the first time

At 10 years old, I took my first trip alone from Boston to New York. That was along about 1915. I'd been visiting Cousin Hannah, one of my father's family, and as she put me on the noon train she said: "Thy father will meet thee. Since thee's in the parlor car, thee'll be perfectly safe. Just read thy book and do not speak to strangers."

My seat was the first one at the end of the car, right across from the drawing room. The door was open and I peeked in.

"Look, Cousin Hannah!" I exclaimed. "A little room! I wish I had this!"

"Lower thy voice," she admonished me. "Drawing rooms are for large families. People do not travel alone in drawing rooms unless they are extravagant."

In my experience Quakers had no dealings with extravagance. As the train pulled out I turned away from the sight of Cousin Hannah, in her mole-gray hat, waving goodbye. I rolled the lovely, forbidden word around in my mouth. I yearned for extravagance. To waste a whole day, to buy something useless, to be kissed for no reason! There were people who lived like that, but not in our family.

As the train stopped at Back Bay Station I looked out at the crowd waiting on the platform, and particularly at a circle of men and women clustered around a fat man. The women were pretty, with bright hats and white gloves, and flowers pinned to their muffs. Most of the men had glossy mustaches. The fat man wore an overcoat that was plainly extravagant—it had a fur collar. None of my father's coats ever had a fur collar.

The fat man was kissed and slapped on the back and hugged. Everyone was laughing and gay. As I watched, I was aware of a procession of bags being carried into the drawing room. For a large family, I thought. The fat man sprang nimbly onto the train step. A woman unpinned the violets from her muff and tossed them to him as the train began to move.

I looked at the drawing room to see the large family, but no one except the fat man went into it. Then the porter came along. Cousin Hannah had given him a tip to take good care of me, so he stopped by my seat.

"You know who's in there, little girl?" he asked, nodding at the closed door.

"No. Who?"

"Mr. Caruso, the opera singer. You ever heard of him?"

"Oh, yes!" I said, looking spellbound at the closed door. We had a victrola and I was allowed to play my father's Red Seal records on rainy afternoons. When the voice called Caruso sang to me I shivered all over.

The porter had disappeared and the passengers weren't watching me. Quickly, before prudence could speak, I slipped out of my chair and tapped at the closed door.

"Come in!" roared an enormous voice. I went in and shut the door quietly. Mr. Caruso was arranging playing cards on a table in front of him. I was astonished. In our house only the cook played cards.

"So, a little girl!" Mr. Caruso glanced up briefly and went on with the cards. "You want my autograph?"

"No, I wanted to see you."

Mr. Caruso slapped the cards down. "You do *not* want my autograph?" he exclaimed.

"What is an autograph?" I asked.

"My name written on a paper."

"What do you do with it?"

Mr. Caruso exploded into laughter, and the drawing room shook.

"How do I know?" He spread his hands and rolled his eyes. All of him was laughing. "Show it, sell it, burn it up. Sit down, sit down. We have five hours to waste. We will play cards."

I slid into the seat across from him. "I don't know how," I confessed.

"No cards, no autograph! What do you do?"

"I go to school."

"Of course. But that is not the whole of life, to go to school. You go to the opera, perhaps?"

"My gracious, no!"

"So, why this 'my gracious'?"

"In our house children don't."

"And what kind of house is this?" he asked.

"My father's a Quaker."

"A what?"

"A Quaker, a Friend."

"To be a friend, this is wonderful. But may not friends go to the opera or play cards?"

"No. Friends are quite strict. I mean you're not supposed to have too much fun. The cook plays cards, but she's Catholic."

"I, too." Mr. Caruso began laying one card on another. "It must be Puritans, this religion of no cards. Would you like me to teach you, little Puritan?"

"Oh, yes!" I exclaimed, looking straight into the painted face of Extravagance. She nodded and smiled at me, only it was Mr. Caruso who smiled. He pulled a second deck out of the bag beside him.

"So!" He handed me the cards with a flourish. "These are for you. Now watch what I do."

After an hour we were playing double Canfield. From time to time Mr. Caruso asked a question about life in a Quaker household. I told him about the silent Meeting and how opera was all right for grown-ups, but children were supposed to improve their minds and go to bed on time. He shook his head at that and began to talk about himself. My head was spinning with new words—Aïda, Rigoletto, Naples, Carmen, Pagliacci …

"You've heard me sing?" he asked, putting a black nine on a red 10.

"Only on a victrola."

"What did I sing for you?"

"*La donna è mobile*."

"Shall I sing it for you now?" he asked.

"Please!"

He put the two and three of spades on the ace and, without looking up, began to sing. His voice was overpowering. It was like having a waterfall leap into my face. I could hardly breathe. The drawing room was swirling with sound, and the sound made color and the color made light and into the light strode giant figures. I was caught up in something I had never known existed. Suddenly it stopped.

"The ace, put out the ace." A fat forefinger jabbed at my cards. I stared at them blankly.

"I forgot," I said.

Mr. Caruso looked pleased. "I made you forget," he said. "I make you forget again."

All that trip he sang and played Canfield and supervised my playing. Sometimes, when he was choosing between two moves, the singing dropped to an undertone. Sometimes it swelled until I thought the drawing-room door would burst open. I was too young and ignorant to know what I was hearing. I only knew that he was making glorious, extravagant pictures with his voice. Men boasted, fought, laughed and wept. Banners waved at high noon. The smell of roses was sweet in the air. Lovers clung together in the moonlight, and I was part of it all.

It was dark as we approached New York. Mr. Caruso stopped singing and peered out of the window into the distance. "Hell Gate," he announced and swept his cards together. "A bad word?" He laughed and rang for the porter. "Bring in the little girl's hat and coat. Who's meeting you?"

"My father."

"The Quaker father!" Mr. Caruso chuckled. "We will surprise him, this Mr. Quaker." He helped me into my coat and buttoned it gently under my chin.

When I Met Caruso

He turned my brown hat around in his hands, disapproval on his face. "So plain," he muttered. "Like the mouse," he added sadly, setting it on my head.

"It's bad taste to be fancy," I quoted primly.

"Ha!" Mr. Caruso spat out the sound of contempt.

When we got off the train in Grand Central, Mr. Caruso stood smiling—hat atilt, debonair, foreign, extravagant—to be photographed. Then he took my hand and swept me up the ramp. As we came through the gate there was a blaze of glory around us. I saw my father standing a little in front of the other people waiting to meet the train. He looked at Mr. Caruso indifferently at first, then sharply, and called, "Elizabeth!"

I tugged at Mr. Caruso's hand. "My father," I said, sandwiched between two titans. Mr. Caruso turned—an extravagant turn, tilted hat, fur collar, all that coat. People stood still to watch.

"Ah, Mr. Quaker!" His voice was so big it filled the station, yet it wasn't loud. "I bring you back your little Puritan. We have spent our afternoon at the opera. When she plays cards with your cook, do not punish her. I myself taught her to play! And I beg you, buy her a hat with flowers!"

Before my father could answer, Mr. Caruso was off. I looked up nervously, expecting to see my father's face black with anger. Instead he was laughing.

"Wonderful fellow!" he said as we got in the cab.

"I thought thee'd be angry," I said, puzzled.

"What about?"

"I spoke to a stranger. I played cards. And Mr. Caruso is extravagant. He had a drawing room all for himself, and Cousin Hannah says that is extravagant."

"Thy Cousin Hannah," said my astonishing father—kissing me for no reason at all, kissing me and throwing open the gates to all lovely adventure—"thy Cousin Hannah is a narrow-minded old woman!"

Originally published in July 1955 issue of *Reader's Digest* magazine. A *Reader's Digest* "First Person Award" winner.

WHERE, OH WHERE?

Turnip Rock

Thousands of years of erosion, along with the trees on top, have made this massive rock resemble a root vegetable, hence its name: Turnip Rock. The shallow water around it allows visitors—who kayak 3½ miles into the lake to see it—to rest before paddling back. And three-quarters of the calls that the local chamber of commerce receives are about Turnip Rock. Where is it?

    A. Acadia National Park, Maine

    B. Grand Marais, Minnesota

    C. Port Austin, Michigan

    D. Coeur d'Alene, Idaho

Answer on page 287. Photograph by Posnov/Getty Images

CREATE A HOME THAT YOU LOVE

"Fill your home with things you love, not things you think other people will love." That was something my mom always said. My home is full of flowers, rabbits, birds, nature, lovely fabrics and elegant glassware. Others tell me it's beautiful, comfortable and welcoming. But everything in it brings me joy, and that's what matters.

—Becca Brasfield, *Burns, TN*

SEE THE WORK

My mom was a woman of few words, but one phrase of hers that stuck was "see the work," which meant see what needs to be done without being told. If toys are left out, put them away. If dishes are being washed, grab a towel and dry. If litter is strewn along the road, pick it up as you walk. I've shared "see the work" with countless students, and our halls are always clean and the chairs stacked by the end of the day. Simple advice from a quiet woman.

—Wendy Baures, *Fountain City, WI*

Your Mom Said *What?*

by Marc Peyser

Does your mother have a habit of saying things she shouldn't? Then you will surely enjoy this fond and funny collection of "mamapropisms."

Whe were new to the neighborhood, so my parents invited a few couples over to play bridge. Pleasantries were exchanged, families were discussed, backgrounds compared.

"You're from New England!" my stepfather, a proud Connecticut Yankee, declared when he detected a telltale accent from one of the men.

"Yes," the man said, "but I bet you can't guess where my wife is from."

The woman in question smiled broadly, but before she could speak to offer a snippet of her own regional locution, my mother piped up with the answer: "She must be from Scotland," Mom said, "because the Scots have terrible teeth!"

Indeed, the woman was from Scotland, though the truth did not set my stepdad free from his embarrassment. My mother has always had a tendency to blurt out information that other people would keep to themselves. It's not that she's mean—far from it. It's just that, like a blender without a lid,

PANTS ON FIRE. I confided that I was discreetly looking into other teaching positions while still employed by my current school district. Mom warned me, "Now, don't go burning your britches behind you!"

—HELENE RAE WISE *SAN YSIDRO, CA*

TWISTED SANDWICH WISDOM. My mother would always say "Mind your PBJs" when she meant to say "Mind your p's and q's."
—**KATHRYN SCHULLER** *PORT ST. LUCIE, FL*

she doesn't have the proper tool to keep her thoughts from spraying all over the room.

Alas, this is something of a hereditary trait in our family. Her mother also provided uncensored insights to people. When I turned 16, she generously offered to pay for me to get my nose fixed. Thanks anyway, Grandma!

People always laugh when I tell them stories about my family's silver tongues, but they invariably have their own tales. So we at *Reader's Digest* decided to collect readers' favorite stories. Some of them are accidental zingers, like my mom's. Others are language mix-ups that produce a sort of sweet word salad. Think of them all as a tribute to helpful moms everywhere. We even gave them a name: *mamapropisms*, after the inimitable literary character Mrs. Malaprop. Come to think of it, she was probably a mother too.

NOT DRESSED FOR SUCCESS

I always sat in the front row during rehearsals of the church choir, but when it was time for our big performance, I was sent to the back row. Dejected,

---

MY, HOW YOU'VE CHANGED! One day, my mother ran into a woman who said they had gone to high school together. Mom insisted she didn't remember her. So the woman came to our house with her yearbook. She pointed out her photo and then my mother's. "Well, of course I didn't recognize you!" Mom said. "You were pretty back then!"

—DEBBIE HAAKENSON *ANCHOR POINT, AK*

WHITE-COAT SYNDROME. Unless she is "near death," as she puts it, my mom refuses to go to the doctor. Recently, she noticed her doctor at a church reception. The man nodded and smiled at her, and she walked over to join him at the dessert table.

"I really need to call you for a visit," she confided. "I know it's been a while." He nodded knowingly, and she leaned closer to whisper into his ear, "You know, I would come see you more often if you wouldn't ask me to take off my clothes every time."

A red flush crept up the man's neck, and he shook his head and smiled. "I believe you must have me confused with someone else," he said. "Perhaps your doctor?"

—JAN SEMPLE MCKINNEY *PARIS, TX*

I relayed my woes to Mom. She said, "Honey, it wasn't because you can't sing. It's because you don't know how to sit in a dress." Somehow, that made me feel better.

—Ernestina Holt *Plainfield, IN*

MESSY RUNS IN THE FAMILY

Sometimes my mother would surprise us by visiting our house on Sundays after Mass. I was a busy mom with my own business and six children still at home. Housework was not at the top of my to-do list. One Sunday, my adult son, Dan, was also visiting. When Mom remarked that she hadn't yet seen his apartment, he told her to let him know when she would like to see it so he could clean.

"I'd be embarrassed to have you just drop by," Dan said. "It can be a real mess."

"Worse than this?" she blurted.

—Mary Potter Kenyon *Dubuque, IA*

WAIT—SHE REALLY IS A GOOD GIRL!

My preteen daughter and I were out shopping. I called her over to where I was, and she responded with the same thing she always said whenever I needed her for something: "Just a sec!"

I didn't even think before I called back, "No more secs for you, young lady. Get over here right now!" Big oops as soon as it left my mouth—and I noticed that people had turned around to stare at us.

—Bonnie Skinner *Dyersburg, TN*

RUNNING INTO TROUBLE

When my brother, my sister and I were little kids and we ran around outdoors, my mom would say, "If you fall down and break your legs, don't come running to me!"

—Kathy Milici *Newton, NJ*

STOP THE PRESSES

My husband had just opened a printing business. He called it Alpha

DISASTER PROOF. Mother was a champion worrier. It didn't matter how much my siblings and I tried to reassure her. "Worrying works!" she liked to say. "Look at all the things I've worried about that never happened."

—**ELAINE BENTON** *HURST, TX*

Thermography because he specialized in thermography, a type of raised print. One day I overheard my mom telling one of her friends, "It's called Alpha Pornography."

—Janice Seidner *Knoxville, TN*

THE FIRST NATIONAL BANK OF MOM

My mom spoke very little English. When I was going through my rebellious teenage years, I would often taunt her with the retort, "Leave me alone!" One day, I overheard her commiserating with a friend. "All my daughter ever says to me is 'Give me a loan, give me a loan!'"

—Kris Karaban *Highland Mills, NY*

WHAT WILL THE NEIGHBORS SAY?

When my mother did her laundry on a sunny day, she liked to hang her wash on a clothesline in the backyard. I was on the phone with her when an unexpected shower popped up. She said to me, "I have to go. It's starting to rain, and I have to go outside and take off my clothes."

—Sandra Youse *Bethel Park, PA*

Originally published in May 2019 issue of *Reader's Digest* magazine.

It's the job of scientists
to explore black holes
in the universe, but
the job of a poet is to
explore black holes
in the psyche.

—SANDRA CISNEROS,
Poet in *Literary Hub*

A Girl, a Seal and the Sea

by Per Ola and Emily D'Aulaire

*Doing what it takes to make
a young pup self-sufficient*

To 17-year-old Katrine Berge, the round silhouette atop the barren islet off Norway's west coast looked like just another sea-scrubbed rock. Then it moved. "Go closer," she urged her father, who was piloting their small boat.

Grabbing binoculars, Katrine focused on a baby seal, no bigger than a puppy. "Why is it alone, Papa?" she asked.

"It might have been abandoned," 43-year-old Trygve Berge answered, turning the boat toward the island where the family—including Katrine's mother, Anny, and 12-year-old brother, Kristian—was spending weekends. "As soon as we're home I'll call the Ålesund Aquarium and ask if there's anything we can do."

While her father telephoned, Katrine continued to peer through binoculars at the helpless pup, and her heart went out to it. Her father interrupted her thoughts. "The aquarium director said to leave the seal there for two days in case the mother returns. If she doesn't, we're to bring it to him so he can examine it."

49

Katrine could hardly sleep the next two nights. When she and her father finally returned to the islet, the seal did not stir. Crawling on hands and knees, Katrine inched forward. "Don't be afraid," she whispered. "We're going to help you."

The seal's dark-gray fur was covered with large, light-brown spots. The dark liquid eyes were oversized, the ears barely visible as two little holes. Beside the right ear was a distinctive white mark, shaped like a star. The seal's nose was rubbery, with a bristle of stiff whiskers.

> *"Don't be afraid," she told the tiny pup. "We're going to help you."*

When Katrine held out her hand, the pup licked her fingers. The girl scooped the furry bundle into her arms, and it settled against her like a sleepy child while they made their way to the aquarium.

There director Jan Einarsen told them, "We've got a robust, 18½-pound male harbor seal here. The question is, what do we do now?" Einarsen explained that the pup could neither feed nor defend itself, so returning it to the sea would mean certain death. Someone would have to take its mother's place for the three months a young seal needs to become self-sufficient.

"Why can't *we* raise the pup, Papa?" Katrine asked. Berge thought for a moment, then told his daughter, "If we take him on, it would be only until he's able to go back to his own kind. We're not going to turn a wild animal into a pet."

Einarsen had more advice: "You'll have to feed him every four hours and keep records of his size and teach him to swim and catch fish. And then, once you've become attached to him, you'll have to let him go." Katrine answered without hesitation: "I'm willing to try, no matter how hard it will be."

Einarsen showed Katrine how to mix in a blender a thick, oily gruel of herring chunks and sea water as a substitute for mother's milk. Then they worked a flexible rubber tube down the pup's gullet and fed some of the gruel into it. The seal settled back as his stomach filled with food. Katrine named him Selik.

"It's important that you are the main one to do the rearing," Berge told his daughter on the way home. "That way the process will be closest to a wild upbringing."

*   *   *

Flipper Power. "This is your home for now," Katrine told Selik as she carried him into their summer house on the island. He nosed at her hands, and she nuzzled his smooth head. He smelled like the sea: salty and fishlike. When Katrine crawled into bed, Selik was soon sound asleep on the floor beside her.

By the end of the first week, Katrine was exhausted. She had to feed Selik four times a day; she had to put salve on his stomach when it got infected; she had to clean up his dung off the floor and scrub him down with soap and water. But Selik seemed to thrive, eagerly exploring his new environment, using his flippers to propel himself into a gallop.

When Katrine finally penned him in the boat shed, Selik protested, barking indignantly. But each morning thereafter, when Katrine went to the shed, Selik greeted her happily. His voice sounded like a cross between a foghorn and a rusty hinge.

Selik was always hungry. At the sound of the blender, he lumbered into the kitchen and opened his mouth wide so Katrine could push the feeding tube down his throat.

"Just my luck," Katrine thought. "A seal that's afraid of the water!"

In the house, Selik followed her everywhere, his front flippers slapping loudly as he pulled himself awkwardly along the wooden floors. Anything that moved fascinated him. He chased his tail like a puppy and batted at strings like a kitten. When Katrine scratched him under the chin he arched his back with ecstasy, almost touching it with his nose. Then, suddenly, he'd rest his chin in her cupped hand and fall asleep.

Outside, Selik rolled in the tall grass, nibbled the wildflowers and chased after butterflies. When Berge mowed the lawn, the pup lurched back and forth in front of the mower as if challenging a rival.

Getting Selik to take his first swimming lesson was a different story. Katrine had to wade into the cove and pull him in. Selik immediately scrambled ashore and bounded for the house. *Just my luck*, Katrine thought.

A seal that's afraid of the water!

Katrine persisted, taking Selik to the cove every day. "The ocean will be your home one day," she told him. Bit by bit, he began to enjoy his daily swims.

When Selik was three weeks old, Katrine figured he was ready for an excursion in the open ocean. "You've seen my world," she told Selik as she assembled her scuba gear. "Now it's time to explore yours."

Katrine sank below the surface of the icy waters, then took hold of one of Selik's flippers and pulled him under with her. At first the pup stayed close by, cautious of the unknown expanse of ocean. Then instinct took control and Selik shot off, twisting and turning, amazing Katrine with his speed and grace. She marveled, too, that he could remain underwater for minutes at a time. As an adult, he would be able to stay submerged up to 20 minutes and swim at 20 miles per hour.

By five weeks, Selik had learned to eat whole fish—but only if Katrine pushed them head first into his mouth. Since the growing seal polished off nine or 10 fish a day, Katrine and her father were kept busy angling. It was time to nudge Selik toward catching fish on his own.

> **By five weeks, Selik had learned to eat whole fish—but only if Katrine pushed them head first into his mouth.**

At Einarsen's suggestion, Berge set up a large plastic tank that Katrine filled with seawater. Then she dumped in a bucketful of plump live salmon, picked Selik up and plopped him in too. At first he tried to chase all the fish at once, darting from one to another. When he finally snagged one, he couldn't figure out what to do. So he let it go.

* * *

Surf Trouble. Selik was growing stronger every day. "Let's take him offshore and see how he handles currents," Katrine told her father.

The sea was unusually choppy when they took the pup out to the rocky islet where they had found him almost two months earlier. Selik didn't seem to mind. He draped his front flippers over the bow and peered ahead eagerly as the boat slapped against the waves.

Katrine clambered ashore on the islet with Selik in her arms. But he was in trouble as soon as she launched him into the water. He was being tossed around dangerously by the crashing waves. Because a seal's skull is its most vulnerable part, Katrine worried that Selik's head would be bashed against the rocks. She tried to call him back, but in vain. Helplessly, Katrine watched the seal struggle in the surf for almost an hour.

Finally, in one lucky moment, Selik caught a breaker and rode it onto the ledge. Katrine grabbed a flipper before the wave could wash him out again. She hugged him with relief. "Oh Selik," she said. "We almost lost you. I guess you have some more growing to do before we try that again."

At 2½ months Selik weighed over 100 pounds, nearly half his adult weight. Katrine could no longer pick him up. He had learned to handle the waves, yet he still hadn't mastered fishing.

Suddenly, in mid-September, Selik began showing signs of his wild heritage. Swimming in tight circles one afternoon in the fish tank, he snagged a salmon as he had countless times before. But this time, instead of letting it go, he flipped it and swallowed it head first. He looked flabbergasted—and pleased. Katrine was exultant. "He *did* it, Papa! He finally caught his own dinner." It was a bittersweet moment, however, for Katrine knew their time together was drawing to a close.

There was one final step in the education of Selik—catching fish in the sea, where his prey could escape. Katrine and Berge rigged a net across the mouth of the cove where Selik had learned to swim. Then Katrine dropped in live fish. The seal nabbed one, then another, as if he'd been doing it all along. Katrine now knew that Selik was almost ready to go.

On a late September afternoon, Katrine and Berge removed the net. Holding back tears, Katrine reminded herself that this was the goal she'd been working toward. "Go on, Selik," she urged. "You're as ready as you'll ever be."

Even with the last barrier to freedom gone, Selik paddled in slow circles near Katrine's dangling feet, brushing against her. Finally Berge pushed him with his rubber boot, propelling him away from shore. Selik hesitated, then swam slowly toward the open sea, pausing several times to look back. When his head was only a small dot in the distance, Katrine and Berge watched him duck beneath the surface and disappear.

Katrine lingered on the rock, hoping for a final glimpse. "Come, Katrine," her father urged gently. "Let's go so he's not tempted to return. You should be very proud."

Katrine climbed to the top of the hill behind the house, tears streaming. She pulled her blue parka tightly around her and gazed out over the sea. Only when the sun sank beneath the horizon did she cease her vigil. "Goobye, Selik," she called, looking out over the darkening water one last time.

Originally published in September 1994 issue of *Reader's Digest* magazine.

In April 1993, more than a year and a half after Selik swam to freedom, Katrine and her father were cruising near their summer island. Katrine called out the seal's name, and suddenly a small brown head popped out of the water. Katrine recognized Selik immediately. He looked sleek and healthy.

She called his name again. The seal pulled himself chest-high out of the water, then swam closer, as if awakened by some dim memory. Then his wild nature took over again. He slipped beneath the water and vanished.

Since then, Selik, with the distinctive mark by his right ear, has been spotted several times in the offshore fishing grounds, frolicking happily in the waves.

Lost Beneath the Mountain

by Per Ola and Emily D'Aulaire

An exciting trip into an abandoned mine turns disastrous when one camper fails to return

Whe n John Skinner, a 43-year-old chemical-plant foreman, drove up to his house in Tooele, Utah, west of Salt Lake City, his wife, Chris, greeted him with ominous news. "There's a boy lost in Hidden Treasure Mine." A 10-year-old had become separated from his companions and hadn't been seen for more than 18 hours. He didn't even have a flashlight.

A kid alone in the dark inside Hidden Treasure! The thought sent shivers down Skinner's spine. His grandfather had been mining superintendent there in the 1950s. As a boy, Skinner had explored every inch of the mine in the Oquirrh Mountains behind his home. Skinner pictured its 21 miles of tunnels sprawling over six levels, its deep pools of stagnant water and its thousand-foot-deep shafts. He knew that cases of old dynamite, so unstable they could explode if someone bumped against them, were strewn about the mine.

Skinner headed for the sheriff's office. "I know Hidden Treasure like my own backyard," he told the dispatcher. "I'd like to help."

The man had orders not to let anyone without rescue credentials join the search. "Thanks, but we have plenty of trained people," he told Skinner. A quiet, unassuming man who dislikes contention, Skinner wasn't about to argue. "Hope you find him soon," he muttered as he left.

*　*　*

The day before, Friday, September 22, 1989, a group of 30 Boy Scouts from Salt Lake City's Troop 845, along with 11 adult leaders, had arrived at the abandoned mine site for a weekend camping trip. The Scouts set up tents and built a fire near a hole that led into Hidden Treasure.

After dinner, the boys pleaded for a quick look inside, and Scoutmaster Kevin Weaver, unaware of all the dangers that the mine held, gave in. Around 7:30 p.m., a group led by Weaver squeezed through the three-foot-wide opening. Shortly after, Scout leader Terry Dennis followed with a second group, which included his son, Josh.

Holding a flashlight high, Dennis kept the boys in sight while lighting their path. When they were several hundred feet inside, one of the Scouts in Dennis's group became frightened and wanted to go back. Dennis saw the lights of Weaver's contingent ahead. "The rest of you catch up with Mr. Weaver," he told the boys. "I'm taking Danny out."

Josh paused, watching his father's light recede. As he turned to follow his friends, he saw only blackness. He looked back in the direction his father had gone. More blackness. "Dad!" he shouted. "Where are you?" The twists and turns of the tunnels muffled his cries. All he heard was a steady drip of water.

*　*　*

Dennis settled by the mine entrance to wait for the others. When Weaver's group emerged almost an hour later, Josh was not with them.

"Where's Josh?" Dennis shouted, suddenly apprehensive.

"I thought he went with you," Weaver said.

"Have we lost him?" Dennis screamed.

"Maybe Josh came out by himself," Weaver replied. The group fanned out through the underbrush, calling Josh's name. Dennis checked the sleeping bags. *I should have kept him with me. What if he's fallen down a shaft?*

✳   ✳   ✳

Deep in the mine, Josh was scared. He tried to remember how many turns there had been coming in. *The entrance can't be too far away*, he told himself. *Maybe I can feel my way out.*

Trailing his right hand along the wall, he was certain he was traveling in a straight line. When he noticed the floor of the tunnel slope upward, he sighed with relief. He remembered a downgrade at the entrance. *I'll be out any minute now.* But the slope steepened. He should have reached the entrance by now.

Sloshing through running water, his hand still following the wall, he moved his feet slowly, wary of anything that felt like a drop-off. He stumbled over rocks and rotting timbers. The slope got steeper. *What do I do now?* he thought. *I must be heading deeper into the mine.*

He groped around a jumble of boulders and sensed he had entered a smaller tunnel. His head bumped the rock overhead. Feeling around the walls, he realized he had ended up in a pocket the size of a tiny room. He was totally lost.

For a moment Josh considered retracing his path down the tunnel. Then he remembered his mother Janeen's advice: "If you're lost, stay where you are." He rubbed his icy hands and stuck them in the pockets of his parka, trying to keep warm. *Please, God, let someone find me soon.*

✳   ✳   ✳

Outside, the youngsters waited, while the adults, armed with flashlights, headed into the tunnel. They divided into teams, checking tunnels and yelling for Josh. After searching the mine with no results, Dennis went to get the sheriff.

Sheriff Don Proctor, a serious man with a determined set to his jaw, alerted the Tooele County Search and Rescue Team and a Salt Lake City search-dog organization. By 4 a.m. more than two dozen members of the rescue team were fanning through the mine. Soon after, the Salt Lake City searchers joined them. They scented the dogs on Josh's sleeping bag and combed the mine, yelling his name.

*   *   *

Josh thought he heard distant voices. "Help!" he yelled. "I'm here. Please help." The tunnels swallowed his calls. Exhausted, he slumped to the floor, leaning against the bumpy rock wall. Shivering in the dank, 50-degree chill, he prayed: *God, please, let me get rescued.* He pulled his parka over himself and drifted into fitful sleep.

*   *   *

When there was still no sign of Josh by Saturday afternoon, word was sent to the boy's mother, and a friend drove her to the site. She remembered the Sunday before Josh disappeared. It had been his turn to give the home evening lesson, a Mormon tradition. He had told his family, "If you have faith, you can do anything." Janeen had said, "You can do *almost* anything." "No, Mom," Josh insisted. "If you have faith, you can do *anything.*" Janeen prayed that this faith was with him now.

*   *   *

Ever since his offer to help was turned down, John Skinner had thought about the boy in the mine. At church on Sunday, he prayed for Josh's safety. After the service he drove to a dirt road that branched toward Hidden Treasure. A deputy stopped him. "I think I can help find that lost boy," Skinner said.

"Sorry," the deputy answered. "We have too many people on the mountain."

Skinner tried again. "I've been in that mine hundreds of times."

The deputy stood his ground. "I've got my orders."

Reluctantly, Skinner drove home. "Somehow," he told Chris, "I'll find a way to get up there."

*   *   *

Josh had no idea if it was day or night. His feet were numb. At times he thought he heard voices or footsteps. He yelled for help, but there was never a reply. He pulled his parka tighter, shivering.

Praying comforted him, Josh discovered. As he drifted off to sleep, he pictured guardian angels hovering over him. A voice inside him spoke: *I will be rescued*.

On Monday morning, Skinner decided to try again. At the roadblock he talked to the deputy who had turned him back. "I know every square inch of that mine," he said. "You've got to let me up there." But he was once more turned away.

Unable to sleep that night, Skinner visualized different areas where the boy might be trapped. A large, mined-out ore body called the Resolute Stope seemed most likely. *Small passageways lead off the stope. Maybe he's in one of those.*

On Tuesday, the fourth day after Josh's disappearance, 15 members of Utah Power & Light's (UP&L) Mine Rescue Team joined the search. The men split into three units and spread through the mine. Their calls met only eerie silence.

Suspecting that Josh might have stumbled out on his own and was wandering in the mountains, Sheriff Proctor mounted a massive manhunt with hundreds of volunteers. While helicopters hovered overhead, horseback riders, all-terrain vehicles and U.S. Army Rangers swept futilely up one side of the mountain and down the other.

Tuesday evening, Skinner watched TV as officials said they believed the mine had been thoroughly searched. To prevent further mishaps, authorities planned to seal the mine off as soon as the rescue effort was abandoned, perhaps the next day.

Skinner was aghast. "They can't do that! He's in there!"

*   *   *

After midnight Sheriff Proctor stopped by the motel where Josh's parents waited. "We're ready to accept the fact that he's dead," Dennis told him. "We just hope you find the body."

On Wednesday morning, Skinner drove up to Hidden Treasure again. The deputy on roadblock duty was a childhood friend who let him through.

Only a handful of people were left. Skinner went to the sheriff and said, "My grandfather used to be superintendent of this mine, and I know a couple of areas that might have been missed. Have you checked the pockets off the Resolute Stope?"

Ray Guymon, leader of the UP&L team, was consulted. "You know what you're talking about," Guymon said. The sheriff agreed to one last effort.

Guymon tossed Skinner a helmet and headlamp, beckoned to his teammate, Gary Christensen, and said, "Let's go." Guymon showed Skinner the spot where Josh and his father had become separated. The trio began searching three areas that Skinner suggested, including the Resolute Stope, without success. When they stopped for a drink of water and to discuss their next move, Guymon heard a noise.

The three men stood motionless. Then they heard a faint, muffled yell. Together they shouted, "Josh! Josh!" Working their way up into the stope, they stopped to holler the boy's name and listen. Skinner heard the cry again.

"I'll stay put so we don't lose the sound," Guymon told the others. "You fan out."

Skinner scrambled in one direction, Christensen in another. Christensen could tell he was drawing closer to the sound. Then it seemed to be behind him, and he backtracked. Suddenly, he spotted a tunnel hidden by boulders. "He's in here!" Christensen shouted, wriggling into the passageway.

"Keep on yelling, Josh," Guymon cried. "Don't move."

But Josh had been sitting still for too long. As Christensen shone the light up the steep passageway, he was met by a cascade of pebbles.

Moments later, a small shape slid toward him feet first. "I've got him!" Christensen called out. Josh clung to Christensen's neck as the miner backed out of the tunnel.

The rescuers were astonished at Josh's composure. He wasn't crying, nor did he seem scared. "The angels comforted me," he explained. "I knew I'd be found."

Skinner scrambled ahead to announce the good news to those

John Skinner with Josh Dennis

outside. "We found him! He's alive!" Pandemonium broke loose as rescuers tossed their hats into the air, yelling and whistling.

Tears rolled down Sheriff Proctor's face. "This is the highest high I've had in 31 years of law enforcement."

Minutes later, at 2:45 p.m., Wednesday, September 27, Guymon and Christensen appeared with the boy. It was over 100 hours after Josh's disappearance—but less than 30 minutes after Skinner entered the mine. Josh was thin and pale, with dark rings around his eyes. His feet were swollen from cold, the skin bulging from his torn sneakers. His mouth was dry; his lips were covered with sores. "I'm a little thirsty," he whispered hoarsely.

*   *   *

Josh's parents were asleep when an urgent pounding on their motel room door jolted them awake. Friends burst in yelling, "He's alive!" Terry and Janeen Dennis rushed to the small hospital where Josh had been taken. "He'll be fine," the doctor assured them. A medical helicopter then whisked Josh to Primary Children's Medical Center in Salt Lake City. Doctors there attributed his extraordinary survival to the temperature in the mine, which had been just cool enough to slow his metabolism and need for water without causing hypothermia or frostbite. Yet Dr. Ted Jenkins, Josh's physician, told the Dennises: "They found him in the nick of time. After five days without water, his kidneys were on the verge of shutting down."

Josh came home two days later, arriving to a celebration of 400 neighbors crowding the streets. Get-well cards poured in from across the country, including one from President Bush.

John Skinner had slipped quietly away from the celebration at the mine site. But now he and Chris arrived at the Dennis home to wish Josh a speedy recovery. "You're the one who saved him," Janeen declared. "You and the men from UP&L." Janeen hugged him; then Terry and Josh did the same. "Thank you for finding me," Josh said. "Thank you for not giving up."

Within a month, Josh's feet had healed, but his ordeal had marked him. "Josh left here a little boy and came back five years older," Janeen says.

Adds Josh, "I know that God answered my prayers and sent me a hero—John Skinner."

Previously hesitant to speak in public, Skinner soon found himself telling the story to 1,200 parishioners in the North Tooele Chapel: "If you want to accomplish anything," he said, "just keep trying and trying and trying. If you have enough prayers, hope and faith, things will work out in the end.

"Miracles do happen, especially when the human spirit kicks in."

Originally published in July 1992 issue of *Reader's Digest* magazine.

Joshua Dennis is a designer and illustrator for The Church of Jesus Christ of Latter-day Saints on Church magazines. He lives in Salt Lake City, Utah, with his wife Johana and their four children.

Creativity lies in the everyday. The great ideas come when you are washing the dishes.

—JIM PARSONS
Actor on the podcast
The Great Creators with Guy Raz

Humor Hall of Fame

There's literally no way to know how many chameleons are in your house.

—@MEGANAMRAM

Once while riding the bus to work, I noticed a man at a stop enjoying a cup of coffee. As we approached the stop, he finished drinking and set the cup on the ground. This negligence surprised me, since it seemed to be a good ceramic cup. Days later I saw the same man again drinking his coffee at the bus stop. Once again, he placed the cup on the grass before boarding. When the bus pulled away, I looked back in time to see a dog carefully carrying the cup in his mouth as he headed for home.

—VALERIE A. HUEBNER

Our grandson has a pet rabbit named Wabbit. One day David came home from school and found that Wabbit had injured a front foot and couldn't walk. He was rushed to the veterinary clinic. After examining Wabbit, the vet returned him to the front desk. Entered on his medical chart was this diagnosis: "Wabbit Gilbert. Wist not bwoken, onwy spwained. Spwint not necessawy."

—ESTHER GILBERT

"While you were away, the dish ran away with the spoon."

When you reach for
your phone first thing
in the morning, it's
like having 100 people
in your bedroom
screaming at you.

–ROBIN ROBERTS,
News Anchor in *People*

The Slave in the Garage

by Mary A. Fischer

Sold by her parents and smuggled into the U.S., one girl did a family's dirty work for two years. And then help arrived.

Like a typical teen, Shyima Hall forgets to make her bed and groans when it's time to do her two chores—vacuuming the floor and cleaning the fishbowl. In the Orange County, California, home she shares with her adoptive parents and five brothers and sisters, the petite 18-year-old lounges on the couch, talking on her cell phone. She wears low-rise jeans, and her nails are painted pink. Last May she went to her prom in a silky gown, her long dark hair worn up with a gardenia. She juggles a packed schedule—part-time job, homework, weekend camp—as if she's making up for lost time.

And she is. A year ago Shyima, who was born in Alexandria, Egypt, closed a chapter in her life she wishes had never been written. It began in 2000, when her impoverished parents sold her to a wealthy couple in Cairo. When the pair moved to the United States, they arranged for the 10-year-old to be brought illegally into the country, where she worked, day and night, in the family's posh home.

*   *   *

According to the U.S. Department of Health and Human Services, human trafficking is a fast-growing criminal industry throughout the world. As many as 800,000 people are trafficked across international borders annually; the United States is a popular destination, with as many as 17,500 people brought in each year and exploited for sex or labor.

"I heard them negotiate, and then my parents gave me away for $30 a month."

Shyima, no stranger to hardship, fell into the latter category. One of 11 children born to desperately poor parents, she grew up in a small one-bathroom house shared by three families. She and her parents and siblings slept in one room on blankets laid out on the floor. Her father was often gone for weeks at a time. "When he was home," says Shyima, "he beat us."

She'd never been to school, and her prospects were bleak. Still, Shyima wasn't without hope. "There was happiness there," she told a courtroom years later. "I had people that cared for me."

When she was 8, she went to live with Abdel-Nasser Youssef Ibrahim and his wife, Amal Ahmed Ewis-Abd Motelib, then in their 30s. Shyima's older sister had worked as a maid for them, but the couple fired her, claiming she'd stolen cash. As part of a deal the couple made with her still-destitute parents, Shyima was forced to replace her.

Two years later, Ibrahim and Motelib decided to move with their five children to the United States to start an import-export business. Shyima didn't want to go. Ibrahim, she says today, "told me I had no choice in the matter." She remembers standing outside the kitchen, overhearing her employers talk with her parents. "I heard them negotiate, and then my parents gave me away for $30 a month to these people," she says.

Shyima was brought into the United States on an illegally obtained six-month visitor's visa and settled into the couple's two-story Mediterranean-style house in a gated community in Irvine. When she wasn't working, she was banished to an 8-by-12-foot section of the garage with no windows, no air-conditioning or heat. Shyima says the family sometimes locked her in.

When Shyima Hall arrived in the U.S. as a slave, "I thought this would be my life forever."

Her furnishings: a dirty mattress, a floor lamp and a small table. Shyima kept her clothes in her suitcase.

Each day she rose at six with the couple's 6-year-old twin boys. She took orders from everyone, including the twins' three sisters, 11, 13 and 15. She cooked, served meals, did the dishes, made beds, changed sheets, helped with laundry, ironed, dusted, vacuumed, swept, mopped and washed the patios, and was often still doing chores at midnight.

One day, when Shyima tried to do her own laundry, Motelib stopped her. "She told me I couldn't put my things in the washing machine because

While Abdel-Nasser Ibrahim (right) and his family lived in luxury, Shyima slept in this windowless room in the garage.

they were dirtier than theirs." From then on, Shyima washed her clothes in a plastic bucket she kept by her mattress and hung them outside to dry on a metal rack, next to the garbage cans.

*　*　*

Motelib and Ibrahim both hit Shyima, but the isolation and verbal abuse were worse. "They called me stupid girl and a nothing," she says. "They made me feel less than them."

She ate alone and wasn't allowed to attend school or leave the house without Motelib or Ibrahim escorting her. The couple warned her against telling anyone about her situation. "They threatened that the police would take me away because I was an illegal," Shyima says.

Though she never admitted longing for her mother, she cried openly in front of Motelib and Ibrahim when she came down with a bad flu. "They saw me suffering and didn't care," she says. "I still had to do my chores. They wouldn't even get medicine for me."

At night, exhausted and lonely, she stared into the darkness. Ibrahim had taken her passport, and she feared she would be held prisoner forever.

When Shyima turned 12, there was no celebration. She spent her birthday doing housework.

*　*　*

Six months later, on the morning of April 9, 2002, Orange County Child Protective Services social worker Carole Chen responded to an anonymous caller (believed to be a neighbor) reporting a case of child abuse. The person said that a young girl was living in the family's garage, acting as a maid and not attending school.

Chen, along with Irvine police investigator Tracy Jacobson, knocked at Ibrahim's front door. When he answered, Jacobson asked who else lived in the house. Ibrahim said his wife and five children.

"Are there other children?" the officer pressed. Ibrahim admitted there was a 12-year-old girl. He claimed she was a distant relative.

"Can I talk to her?" Jacobson asked.

Cleaning upstairs, Shyima was oblivious that her salvation was moments away. Ibrahim called to her in Arabic, telling her to come downstairs and deny that she worked for them. Shabbily dressed in a brown T-shirt and baggy pants, she hurried to the door.

Chen, who noticed that the girl's hands looked red and raw, called a translator on her cell phone. Shyima told him that she'd been in the country for two years and had never been to school.

Officer Jacobson promptly took the girl into protective custody. Riding in the backseat of the police car, headed to a children's group home where she would be temporarily placed, Shyima prayed she'd never have to face her captors again. "She was amazing, a very strong child," Jacobson recalls. "She never cried. Shyima liked being in protective custody, unlike other kids, because she felt safe."

A few hours later, Jacobson, armed with a search warrant, returned to Ibrahim's house with agents from the FBI and Immigration and Customs Enforcement (ICE). In the garage, they photographed Shyima's stained mattress. A bucket of soapy water stood next to a broken lamp; folded clothes were on the floor. "Shyima lived in complete contrast to the rest of the family," says Jacobson. ICE agent Bob Schoch adds, "I've seen pets that are treated better."

Hoping to justify the arrangement, Ibrahim showed the agents the handwritten, notarized contract he and Shyima's mother and father had signed. "It said she was to work for them for 10 years," Jacobson says, "for a stipend paid to her parents of $30 a month."

The investigator arrested Ibrahim and Motelib, charging them with conspiracy, involuntary servitude, obtaining the labor of another person unlawfully and harboring an alien.

*　　*　　*

On the day of Shyima's rescue, immigration officials offered her a choice: Return to Egypt or stay in America and live in a foster home. Nervous and tentative, Shyima phoned her father in Egypt and blurted out, "I want to stay here." He was angry, but Shyima's mind was made up: She wanted to start a new, better life.

During the next two years, she lived with two foster families. In the first

Shyima celebrates with Jenny and Chuck Hall, now her adoptive parents, after testifying at the sentencing hearing for the couple who enslaved her.

home, she learned to speak and read English. In the next one, in San Jose, they expected her to become a strict Muslim, and after an argument, they dropped Shyima off at a local group home. "I just wanted to be a regular American teenager," she says.

She soon got her wish. Chuck and Jenny Hall, parents of two daughters and a son, had recently bought a four-bedroom house in Orange County and decided they had room for more children. After becoming foster parents to a 15-year-old girl and Chuck's 13-year-old nephew, they were ready to welcome another. At their first meeting with Shyima, "we all clicked," says Chuck, a uniform company service manager. "She had the same sense of humor I do."

Shyima had just two questions for her prospective parents: Were there house rules, and what chores would she have to do? "Everything is negotiable," Chuck answered.

"The No. 1 rule: Homework and school first," added Jenny, a youth counselor. "We'll treat you as our own daughter. You'll be part of our family."

By then 15, Shyima had blossomed into a beautiful young woman. But she brought more with her than her suitcase. "I had a whole lot of anger," she says. For the first six months, she had trouble sleeping and suffered from anxiety. She regularly saw a therapist and took medication for depression.

With time, she grew more self-confident. At school, she made friends, including a first boyfriend, and joined the track team. She got a part-time job at a Godiva chocolate store and participated in church dinners and car wash fundraisers. She even volunteered to be a counselor at a camp for children with low self-esteem.

Ibrahim and Motelib, meanwhile, accepted a plea bargain to avoid trial. At their October 2006 sentencing hearing, Shyima sat nervously in the courtroom, listening to their pleas for mercy. "What happened was due to my ignorance of the law, but still I have all responsibility," Ibrahim told the judge.

Motelib was less repentant: "I treated her the same way as I would treat her in Egypt. I would have been very happy if she had come and told me, 'Please don't do this.' Then I would have changed my actions."

Unable to contain her outrage, Shyima asked to address the court. "[Motelib] is a grown woman, so she knows right from wrong," she said. "Where was their loving when it came to me? Wasn't I a human being too? I felt like I was nothing when I was with them. What they did to me is going to scar me for the rest of my life."

Ibrahim received a reduced sentence of three years in prison, and Motelib got 22 months. The couple were also ordered to pay Shyima $76,137 for the work she did. Both will be deported to Egypt when they get out of jail.

*   *   *

After the hearing, Shyima celebrated by going shopping for a dress to wear to her high school homecoming dance. She and Jenny chose a beautiful one—long, shiny and black. With a portion of her restitution money, Shyima also got a laptop, a digital camera and a new Nissan Versa; she put the rest into a college fund.

"She's strong-willed and independent," says Jenny, who with her husband legally adopted Shyima. "She knows what she wants."

As for the future, Shyima says she'd like to be a police officer so she can help other people. She also wants to return to Egypt one day to visit her brothers and sisters. For now, though, she's content, indulging the dream she never imagined would come true: life as a regular American teen.

Originally published in May 2008 issue of *Reader's Digest* magazine.

"YOU'VE GOT MAIL"

Our front door is 50 feet from our mailbox. To eliminate unnecessary trips, I devised the "mail alert." I tied fishing line around a tennis ball, resting it atop the mailbox, then wrapped the line around the mailbox door. When the door is lowered, the string pulls the tennis ball off. If the ball is hanging underneath the mailbox, I know the mail has arrived.

—David Chandler, *Owens Cross Roads, AL*

MIND, SEALED, DELIVERED

I wanted to write back to a friend, but the return address on the envelope he'd mailed to me was nearly illegible. Instead of deciphering it, I cut that portion off his envelope and taped it to the addressee area of a new one. I enclosed my letter, and off it went. Ever since, he's called me the laziest person he knows.

—David Zelinsky, *Towaco, NJ*

"I Love You"

by George H. Grant

The words may not come easily, except to lovers, but there are times when they need to be said

At the end of World War II, I received orders to transfer from the merchant vessel I had commanded for many years. I was packed to leave when the chief mate came to my quarters. Some of the crew were outside and wanted to say goodbye, he reported. A dozen men were on the lower bridge when I reached it. An old oiler stepped from the group. With the swift gesture of embarrassment he thrust a package into my hand. It contained a watch, inscribed: *To Capt. Geo. Grant Who Has Guided Us Safely Through This War.*

A lump as big as a barge choked me as I surveyed the men. They were a mixture of Latin American nationalities: Costa Rican, Panamanian, Honduran. We had crossed and recrossed the Atlantic together, with bombs for Britain. We had zigzagged around the Pacific, delivering Christmas cheer to our armed forces. We had carried provisions to our Naval vessels during the almost catastrophic kamikaze blockade of Okinawa. We had shared danger, loneliness and fear.

When some would have squandered their money on the "wine, women and song" of ports we visited, I had taken most of it from them and sent it to their families. I had "logged" them when they were unfit for duty, and when they had overstayed their leaves. When bombs, shells and torpedoes had come dangerously close, I had cheered them. Now they floated in a mist before my eyes.

"Why did you do this?" I blurted.

The old oiler answered, in Spanish, "We love you, sir."

There was another time, later. An aged friend was dying of leukemia. He had lived an active life as head of a newspaper syndicate, and a convivial social life. As a raconteur and singer of ballads, he had few equals. As a companion, he possessed the qualities of compassion and understanding that are not given to many. He knew he was dying. And yet, as we gathered around the piano at his house one night, he seemed to symbolize the eternity of life.

Suddenly a strange emotion possessed me. Before it could be controlled, I took him into my arms and said, "Gosh! I love you." He stiffened in my embrace as a man will when another man puts his arms around him. I thought he would push me away. Then a solitary tear ran down his cheek, and he relaxed. He punched me playfully in the stomach, as was his habit. "You old faker, you," he said.

Next morning he phoned me from the bed that was to be his deathbed within a month. "I have felt that way at times," he said quietly. "Never could let go. Wish I had. Too late now. I love you, you old faker, you."

We have three grandchildren—Anne, Pam and Randy, ages 6, 4 and 3. Part of their summer vacation is spent in our house. Every morning they come down, each in turn, and I give them breakfast. Anne is a restless wee thing, silent, introspective, shy. Only in the early morning do I become her confidant. Through a mouthful of cereal she asked one day, "How old must I be to be engaged?" Her question took me aback. Six! What long, long thoughts were running through her head?

I quibbled. "People get engaged at almost any age," I said. "Who's your boyfriend?" She mentioned a boy who lived nearby. He was 14, interested in boats and swimming. Girls, of his age, he shunned like the plague. "Why don't you ask him?" I suggested. She sought my sincerity with a penetrating look. "He might laugh at me, Granddad," she said.

He wouldn't, for I would tip him off. "Ask him, Anne," I suggested again.

Anne lapsed into silence. When she had finished her breakfast, she threw her arms around my neck. She hugged me with that affection only a child can give. "I love you, Granddad," she said, and went skipping down toward the bay, happiness in every skip.

I LOVE YOU. Three wonderful words that come easily to the lips of lovers, but often cling to the tongues of others when they should go free.

I LOVE YOU. Three words that hold so much of gratitude, understanding and faith. They should be said.

Originally published in May 1962 issue of *Reader's Digest* magazine.

Humor Hall of Fame

Being a good husband is like being a stand-up comic. You need 10 years before you can even call yourself a beginner.

—JERRY SEINFELD

My younger brother and his wife celebrated their first anniversary, and they invited the family for dinner. The conversation focused on how they met. The men related how we'd met our wives. Everyone told his story but my youngest brother. He said, "Oh, Cindy and I met in college. We were matched up by a computer according to compatibility." "That's the whole story?" my wife asked. "Oh, no," he grinned. "They've fixed the computer since."

—JOHN MORRISSEY

After Adam stayed out late a few nights, Eve became suspicious. "You're running around with another woman—admit it!" she demanded. "What other woman?" Adam shot back. "You're it!" That night, Adam was fast asleep when he was awakened by Eve poking him in the chest. "What are you doing?" "Counting your ribs."

—WILLIAM HALLIDAY

"It's about time."

P. BYRNES

In the Jaws of a Polar Bear

by Robert Kiener

When two best friends took off on a two-month kayak trip north of the Arctic Circle, they expected the adventure of a lifetime. They got that—and more.

The massive polar bear lumbered along the rocky shoreline, just a yard or so from the stormy waters of the Arctic Ocean. Occasionally it raised its head to sniff the Arctic air, hoping perhaps to pinpoint an easy meal of a washed-up ringed seal or walrus carcass.

It was late July, and in this uninhabited part of the Norwegian archipelago of Svalbard, high above the Arctic Circle and just 600 miles from the North Pole, much of the drift ice had melted. This made hunting for seals—a polar bear's favorite meal—nearly impossible. Although huge, the bear was desperately hungry.

With a westerly wind at its back, the male bear continued to patrol the shore. Then, perhaps catching the scent of something unusual, it stopped dead in its tracks. It sniffed the air, and steam billowed out of its bright black snout. Following its nose, so sensitive that some say it can smell a decaying whale carcass from 20 miles away, the bear suddenly turned downwind

At 11 years old, the polar bear was 800 pounds and 9 feet tall.

and inland. Its paddlelike paws dragged, leaving deep tracks in the sand. The predator was closing in on its prey.

It was to be the adventure of a lifetime. For almost two years, longtime friends Sebastian Plur Nilssen and Ludvig Fjeld, both 22, had been training for this two-month-long kayak expedition. Hoping to follow in the footsteps of other Norwegian explorers such as Roald Amundsen and Thor Heyerdahl, the two were attempting to become the first kayakers to paddle around the entire Svalbard archipelago, a trip of more than 1,100 miles through one of the world's most remote regions.

To get fit, they had donned dry suits and kayaked through the ice-filled rivers near their hometowns outside Oslo, pulled heavy kayaks over ice floes, and jumped into the freezing waters to toughen themselves.

Lifelong hunters, they honed their marksmanship by sprinting up hills, loading their rifles and pulling the triggers. As many Arctic experts had told them, if they needed to defend themselves from a polar bear,

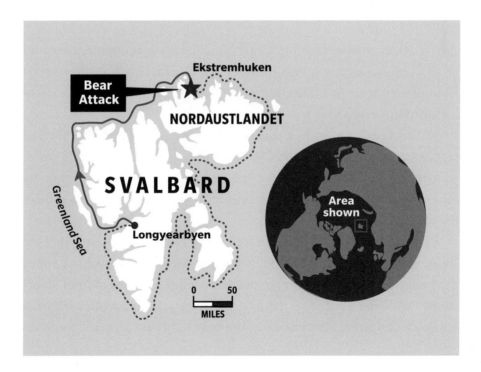

Fjeld (left) and Nilssen hoped to be the first to paddle around Norway's Svalbard archipelago.

they'd have little time to think. Each carried a rifle in a waterproof bag lashed to their kayaks. Holding steady, controlling their breathing, aiming, shooting: It all had to be second nature.

* * *

The two pioneers set out from Longyearbyen, dubbed the northernmost settlement in the world, on July 5, 2010. They averaged about 15 miles a day, and by the end of July, they had reached the northern shore of Nordaustlandet, one of Svalbard's High Arctic islands.

With the wind picking up and the sea growing choppy, they decided to head for shore and camp on a beach near a promontory named Ekstremhuken. As Nilssen paddled alongside Fjeld, he held up the map and joked, "Funny name for a place, no? I wonder if that means something 'extreme' will happen here?" Fjeld smiled.

After pulling their kayaks onto the rocky beach, they pitched their tent and rigged up a trip-wire perimeter nine feet away, as they did at every campsite. A series of small explosive charges would go off if an animal were to cross the wire, giving the men time to grab their rifles and scare away a bear or, if necessary, shoot it.

The two awoke the next day to ferocious winds and rough seas. After checking the weather forecast via satellite phone, Nilssen and Fjeld discussed the situation. "We'll have to stay another night," Nilssen said. "Tomorrow should be clear."

> *Just at the moment the bear seemed about to sink its massive canines into Nilssen, it turned to look at Fjeld.*

Later that day, while chasing a tarp that had blown away, Nilssen fell over the trip wire, setting off an explosive charge. He quickly fitted a new one to the wire.

"Damn," he said as he crawled back inside the tent, "I'm getting clumsy in my old age." As they did every night before they tucked in, Nilssen and Fjeld double-checked that their rifles were loaded and close at hand.

As they were sound asleep, the polar bear that had picked up their scent began lumbering toward the camp.

*   *   *

With the wind howling, the bear burst through the trip wire, but the charge did not fire. Nilssen awoke to a crashing sound when the bear trampled the tent and ripped it to shreds with a mighty sweep of its paw. "Bear!" shouted Nilssen as he felt it lock its jaws onto the back of his skull, pulling him from his sleeping bag. All he could see was a towering mass of white fur. As the bear sank its teeth deeper into his skull, it uttered a low-pitched, guttural growling.

Nilssen was able to grab his pump-action shotgun while the bear dragged him out of the tent. Screaming, he tried to hit the bear with one hand while gripping the gun with the other. But nothing deterred the animal.

Suddenly the polar bear changed its hold on Nilssen and sank its teeth into his right shoulder. Then it shook him back and forth, each time penetrating Nilssen's flesh more deeply with its teeth. Pain shot through his body as if an ice pick were being twisted into his shoulder.

It's trying to shake me unconscious, thought Nilssen. The bear began dragging him onto the rocky beach. *The shotgun is my only chance*, he thought. Just then the gun fell from his grip, and the bear stepped on it, snapping it in two. "I'm dead," Nilssen said out loud when he heard the gun break in half. "It's over."

* * *

Fjeld woke up when he heard Nilssen scream and turned to see the bear inside the tent, with Nilssen's head in its jaws. While shaking him, the bear had stomped on their gear, much of which was now crushed or buried in the soft sand.

Fjeld jumped up and reached for his grandfather's World War II rifle. It was missing. He frantically clawed at the debris in front of the tent. "Where is it?" he yelled, then felt the stock of the rifle and pulled it out of the sand. "Sebastian!" he yelled. Sebastian didn't answer.

The kayakers' camp after the attack

In Norway, it's a crime to shoot a polar bear unless your life is threatened.

The bear was now by turns dragging and carrying Nilssen by his wounded shoulder. *I must act now to save my friend*, thought Fjeld. Time was running out.

The bear dropped Nilssen some 100 feet beyond the camp. Then it roared and raked its razor-sharp claws over Nilssen's torso. Blood covered the kayaker. The bear put its two front paws on Nilssen's chest, pinning him to the ground and pushing him deep into the sand. Nilssen felt his ribs cracking. The bear's hot breath was on his face. He looked directly into its deep black eyes. They were cold and empty.

Then the bear turned and saw Fjeld standing with rifle raised outside the tent. Fjeld held his breath to still his shaking trigger finger and aimed at the bear. "Steady," he repeated to himself. He was afraid he would hit his friend. Nilssen yelled, "Shoot! Shoot!" But before Fjeld could fire, the bear climbed off Nilssen, sunk its jaws into the back of his skull again, and stood straight up, lifting Nilssen several feet off the ground.

Fjeld ran closer to them. Nilssen shouted again, "Shoot! Shoot or I die!"

The polar bear stood sideways to Fjeld; he aimed at its back and squeezed off a shot. The bullet ripped into the bear, and the animal dropped Nilssen to the sand. One last time the bear managed to sink its teeth into Nilssen's shoulder. Then Fjeld pumped four more rounds into the beast's chest. The bear fell over, dead at last.

* * *

Fearful that other polar bears might be attracted by the smell of blood, Fjeld slammed another five-shell clip into the gun. Nilssen lay crumpled on the beach. The back of his scalp hung loose and his shoulder was shredded open. His body was covered with bleeding wounds, but he was alive.

Fjeld carried him back to the tent; he covered his bleeding scalp and shoulder with compression bandages and wrapped him in a sleeping bag. "You'll make it," he told Nilssen as he gently wiped blood from Nilssen's face. "We'll get you out of here."

Nilssen groaned. His body throbbed with pain, and the smell of his blood filled the tent. He whispered to Fjeld, "My neck. I think the bear might have broken it."

* * *

Fjeld knew he had to keep Nilssen warm because it would be hard to survive the frigid temperature with such devastating wounds. He punched the number of a Longyearbyen hospital into the satellite phone. The operator picked up.

"We need help," Fjeld blurted out. "We are kayakers," he told the hospital's nurse manager, Aksel Bilicz. "My friend has been attacked by a polar bear. Please hurry!"

"I know it's common for bears to crush seals' skulls," says Nilssen. "Lucky for me, I'm thickheaded."

Bilicz called the local police, and about 35 minutes later, a rescue helicopter was in the air. The trip to the camp, however, would likely take almost an hour and a half.

Fjeld returned to Nilssen's side. Nilssen was pale and shivering. Fjeld talked to him incessantly to keep him awake. "They are sending a helicopter," Fjeld repeated. "It won't be long." Though Nilssen writhed in pain, Fjeld made the hard decision to withhold a dose of the morphine they carried with them because it might knock Nilssen out. Despite his suffering, Nilssen did not want to lose consciousness. Meanwhile, Fjeld scanned the horizon for other polar bears, his rifle loaded by his side.

When the helicopter touched down, two medics carried Nilssen to the chopper. He was put on a saline drip and given a painkiller, though his neck throbbed too much for a brace.

At the hospital, Nilssen underwent a three-hour operation during which surgeons removed all the damaged tissue under his wounds. His neck was badly bruised but not broken. The next day, as Nilssen lay recuperating, surgeon Kari Schroeder Hansen visited him. "Another few millimeters and the bear's teeth would have punctured your lung and crushed your skull," the doctor told him. "You wouldn't still be with us."

"I know it's common for bears to crush seals' skulls," Nilssen says now. "Lucky for me, I'm thickheaded."

*　*　*

Today, at home north of Oslo, where he is raising a team of sled dogs, Nilssen sips coffee with Fjeld. Nilssen unbuttons his shirt. His shoulder and torso are tracked with scars from the attack. "I'm not a religious person, but I know it was a miracle I survived," he says as he buttons up. "I also know that I owe my life to Ludvig."

Fjeld demurs, saying, "I just instinctively did what we were both trained for."

The men are considering a return expedition to Svalbard—although their families, who initially learned of the attack on a radio program, are not keen on it. When asked about the experience, Nilssen is amazingly composed. "It is our big regret that the bear had to be killed," he says reflectively. "I still think the polar bear is the most majestic animal in the world. It was just trying to survive."

Originally published in March 2011 issue of *Reader's Digest* magazine.

Marriage is the
punctuation mark and
the celebration of what
you already have.

—JULIETTE LEWIS,
Actor in *Slate*

WHERE, OH WHERE?

Giants

And ... action! These fittingly larger-than-life cutouts of James Dean and Elizabeth Taylor as they appeared in their 1956 movie, *Giant*, are hard to miss along Highway 90. The flick lived up to its name in both its runtime (three hours) and its reach: It inspired an enormously popular 1980s TV show. Where is this?

    A. Chipley, Florida

    B. Anniston, Alabama

    C. Ruidoso Downs, New Mexico

    D. Marfa, Texas

Answer on page 287. Photograph by LSchrandt Photography/ Alamy Stock Photo

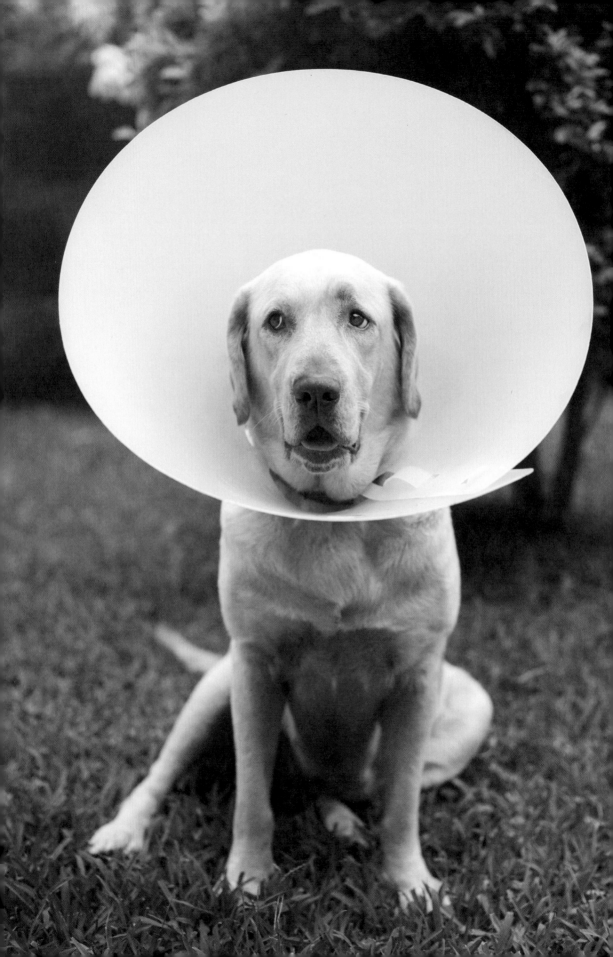

Best Cheap Fun!

by Mary Roach

*Sometimes it is possible to find humor
in the oddest of places, and car keys*

The price of a movie ticket has gone double-digit. You need a major league contract to afford an afternoon at the ballpark. Has fun priced itself out of our lives? Not at all.

Photo booths. While you wait for your strip to be developed, reach up and feel around the top of the booth. People often toss their embarrassing outtakes up there.

BUBBLE WRAP

Your cat. Blow into his face. Stick your finger in his mouth as he yawns. Put him on a leash and try to take him for a walk.

The sight of a dog wearing one of those medical lampshades on its head. For immediate gratification, do a Google image search for "Elizabethan collar," which is what veterinarians call it.

Wave at people while you drive.

HELIUM BALLOONS

The weekly police roundup in any small-town newspaper. I am still laughing over the report of a man seen running naked down a neighborhood street. A policeman who arrived to investigate noticed a note on a car windshield that read "Gone to get parts." The officer misread this as "Gone to get pants" and, satisfied that this explained the man's nudity, returned to his beat.

BUMPER CARS

The commuter ferry on a blustery day. My brother comes to visit me once a year, and if the weather's dramatic, we always head for the ferry dock. Go on the weekend and have the ship to yourself.

Order a dish off the Chinese-language side of the menu.

Any toenail polish color besides red.

BUBBLEGUM

Type "yink" into your spell checker and read the suggestions out loud.

Those 25-cent horsy rides outside the Walmart.

ROOT FOR THE RED SOX AT YANKEE STADIUM.

Request a phony page on the white courtesy telephone. I once heard (in a hospital) "Al Bumin, dial operator. Al Bumin, operator please." Someone in my dorm in London once paged "Mahatma Coat."

Did you know there's a brand of dishwashing detergent in Iran called Barf? Or that Japan sells a sports drink called Pocari Sweat?

Supermarkets in foreign countries.

Launch a message in a bottle with your email address. For maximum exoticism of response, remember to do it when the tide is going out, not coming in.

Lie down in a cow pasture. If the herd is far off, yell to get their attention, then immediately drop down and lie flat. The entire herd will come galloping over and form a tight circle around you, staring down at you with intense bovine curiosity. I have tried this three times on two different continents. It's marvelously surreal.

LATE NIGHT INFOMERCIALS

Armpit farts. Here's a variation that will make you feel less childish (but fools no one). It works best in humid weather. Lie on a wood floor, pull up your shirt and press your slightly damp lower back into the floor as firmly as you can. Then pull away quickly. This is also a good lower-back strengthening exercise, but who cares.

Originally published in May 2007 issue of *Reader's Digest* magazine.

MY LUCKY STRIKE

Years ago, I joined a bowling league. My score rarely broke 100, but one night I threw a ball that popped out of the gutter and knocked down all 10 pins. I was thrilled to have gotten a strike until my teammates told me it didn't count. When we had our awards dinner, I received an award for being the only person to ever get a gutter strike at that bowling alley. Even though it didn't count, I still did something no one else had.

—Lisa Harris, *Shallotte, NC*

A HEADS-UP PLAY

The score was close and the end of our volleyball game near. I dived for a ball but pulled up when I saw another teammate already after it. She bumped it straight up in the air. I leaped to my feet but didn't know where the ball was. Suddenly, the ball hit me—no joke—square on top of the head. It arched up into a perfect set that another teammate spiked over the net. We won the point and the game.

—Susannah Reavis, *Houston, TX*

The Price of Freedom

by Ben Montgomery, from *Gangrey.com*

A recovered account of World War II opens a grandson's eyes to how the sacrifice of one altered the fate of many

The other day I was searching for something behind my desk, and I found an envelope. My dad's funeral, in November 2011, had been kind of a blur, but I remembered a teacher from Kellyville High School, in the rural Oklahoma community near where my dad lived, pushing an envelope into my hands that day. I must've taken it out of my briefcase when I got back, and it had slipped into the crevice between my desk and the wall, unopened.

Now I read the teacher's note on the outside. She explained that inside was a speech given by my grandfather two decades before. He didn't much like talking about the war, but he had agreed to be the school's Veterans Day speaker. The teacher had loved my grandpa, who had died two weeks before my father, and she thought I should have his speech. Her note concluded: *He received an awesome standing ovation, and many tears were shed by guests and students. In loving memory of your grandpa.*

I began reading my grandfather's war story.

My grandfather, Paul Montgomery

*　*　*

In my senior year, in 1941, I was seated about where you are seated. I was 17. Your history books will tell you that on December 7 of that year, the Japanese bombed Pearl Harbor. I enlisted in the Army Air Corps and was commissioned a second lieutenant. I began training to fly the B-29 bomber, and I was stationed in the Mariana Islands in the western Pacific, bombing targets on the mainland of Japan, 1,500 miles away.

On July 19, 1945, we made a bombing run on the Mitsubishi aircraft factory in Osaka, Japan. My good friend Bob Johnson from Minnesota was on another crew, and he was flying on the plane behind us as our wingman. There were 42 planes in the formation, each carrying three 4,000-pound bombs. As we neared the target, the Japanese attack on us began in earnest. It was so heavy I believed you could get out and walk on it.

About 30 seconds from "bombs away," Bob Johnson's plane took a direct hit and exploded. From my limited visibility, I could not see the fate

The Victory Girl, *adorned with the image of "a tastefully dressed beautiful young lady" painted by the right gunner, Milton Gross from Philadelphia*

of the crewmen or their parachutes. I only saw huge pieces of their aircraft fly by. On my plane, we took a hit in our No. 3 engine and headed for home. Home that day was a coral island called Iwo Jima. As we were taxiing in, you could see the price we'd paid for that tiny island—7,000 crosses marked the graves of U.S. Marines and infantrymen along the runway. My heart was heavy, not knowing what happened to Bob. I was 21, and I thought I was tough, but I could hardly see the taxiway because of the tears in my eyes.

Then we had a few days off, and our squadron commander gave us permission to paint a logo on our aircraft. We all voted for the right gunner, Milton Gross from Philadelphia, to paint. He chose the picture of a tastefully dressed beautiful young lady. We called our aircraft the *Victory Girl*.

On September 2, 1945, we flew cover for Gen. Douglas MacArthur as he steamed into Tokyo Bay aboard the USS *Missouri* and signed the declaration of peace with the Japanese. The war was over. I got home Thanksgiving Day.

In 1995, the crew of the *Victory Girl* decided to have a reunion. I was retired, living on a ranch near Slick, Oklahoma. I flew to Pennsylvania, walked into a Holiday Inn conference room, and saw a crew I had not seen in 50 years. We were all wrinkles, baldness, and aches and pains, and we were missing four crew members.

An enlarged picture of our original crew was shown, and I said I'd like to know what had happened to Bob Johnson. I'd been wondering about him all these years. You could have heard a pin drop. A tear fell on the old photograph.

"You don't know, do you?" one of the men asked.

"No," I said. "I couldn't see."

"Well, we saw," he said. "All the chutes came out 'streamers'"—which meant that Bob's plane had been destroyed.

The book was closed on Bob Johnson. At least now I knew.

We went around the room, each man taking time to relate what had happened in the 50 years that had passed. When it was Milton Gross's turn, he passed around pictures of his family. He said when he got home, he enrolled in the Philadelphia Institute of Art. One night, he went to a party. He walked in and saw a beautiful blond-haired, blue-eyed girl, about 20 years old: his real-life Victory Girl.

He introduced himself. They began to date, and in due time, he asked her to marry him. But the real story is how she came to be at that party.

Ten years earlier, when she was 10 years old, she was a Jew living in a small village in occupied France. One night the Germans kicked in the door of her house and found a young mother making supper for a daughter. Her mother was shot point-blank, and the girl was thrown into a German army truck, driven to a prison compound, and tagged for the gas chamber. How you can exterminate a little girl, I don't know.

She was sitting in the barracks on the eve of being sent to a concentration camp when a man came up to her in the darkness and asked her a question. "Are you Sarah Pertofsky?"

She said, "Yes."

The man said, "I'm your uncle, and I have around my neck a green dog tag. I'm a Jew and a machinist, and they are keeping me for work. You have a red dog tag, and that's not good. I'm going to trade tags with you." So he took her tag and placed his around her neck.

"Let's go outside," he said. "I need to show you something." Outside, he pointed to the Big Dipper and how its lip points to the North Star.

"Here's what I want you to do," he said. "I've found a hole in the fence just big enough for a girl to squeeze through. When the guard passes the hole in the fence, I'll push you through, and I want you to put that North Star over your shoulder and keep it there and go. You'll be headed south. I want you to run straight south for three days until you come to a village called Monet. My wife lives there, and she'll take care of you."

In the darkness, they crept to the fence, and as the guard passed, her uncle handed her three crusts of bread that he'd saved, and he pushed her through. Sarah ran

The American cemetery at Iwo Jima

My grandfather (back row, second from left), with his squadron

across the road, hid in a clump of tall grass, and turned and waved goodbye to him. Then she ran and ran and ran, all night long. When morning came, she stopped and licked some dew off the grass and ate one of the crusts of bread. Then she went off again, straight south. She stopped to drink water from a creek but kept going. On the third afternoon, she saw an old farmer hoeing a field. Sarah ran up to him and cried, "Monet? Monet?"

"Yes," he said. "I know Monet."

He brought her to that village, and they found her aunt. The aunt took her in, raised her and put her through school. Sarah was living and working in Philadelphia when Milton Gross walked into that party. The two of them now live there, have three children and enjoy their life together.

What's the price of freedom? All the Bob Johnsons, all those crosses along the taxiway on an island in the Pacific and all the lives lost during that war. They paid for us and paid with their lives. And the uncle and mother of Sarah Pertofsky—they paid the price for a little 10-year-old girl. Oh, what a price. To you, it's free. Hold it high.

Originally published in July/August 2017 issue of *Reader's Digest* magazine.

Goodbye to Shamrock

by Frederic A. Birmingham

Even after an absence of only a few moments, he greeted me as if I had been away for years. And now he's gone forever.

He was a miniature white poodle and his registered name was Snowdrift Highstepper of Greenglade. But we called him Shamrock because he was born on St. Patrick's Day. True to his name, he was blithe and gay, and he graced wherever he visited simply by being there.

Yesterday was his last. It was I who had to give the order for his execution, and afterward I buried him. Those who have their own Shamrocks will understand why I am not ashamed of my tears and why I have been driving my car very badly, now that he is gone. I think I see Shamrock behind every tree. Last night when I found a rubber band on the floor of my study I picked it up with great relief, at the thought of discovering it before Shamrock found it and accepted the challenge of perpetual gnawing. Until I remembered.

Shamrock had been destined for high glory in the show ring by his forebears. But after he had had a few puppy triumphs, he slipped out of the house one day and was run over by a delivery truck. Our veterinarian found that Shamrock had numerous compound fractures in the rear of his body, and he was twisted and torn in a dozen other ways. After a long operation the doctor shook his head. I looked at Shamrock's battered body and said that I would like to try and keep him alive, even though the doctor warned me Shamrock had probably lost the use of his hind legs and that his tail would never wag again.

Yet yesterday, when Shamrock died, he was 12 years old, and even at the last, the stub of a pompon on his stern wagged once again so furiously as to justify his third name of Old Propeller Tail.

In the first months after his operation he could only pull himself along the ground a little at a time by his front paws. It seemed impossible that he could ever make it. But he did, thanks to the lion's heart in him. I would set him on the steep hill up among the small pines, and free his splinted, bandaged hind legs a little as I faced him downhill. After a while he learned how to move them to keep his balance. Then he began to walk on level ground too. Finally I could walk uphill slowly with Shamrock laboring after me. In the end, he ran like a breeze again.

Some might call it a triumph of medical science. But I know that it was actually a triumph of the will to live.

Shamrock was gentle in manner, an aristocrat who ate his food as cleanly and daintily as any duchess. He had only one dog fight, but in his own eyes it was victory enough for a lifetime. A rather nasty customer of a collie was chewing up a beagle in front of our house one day, so I went out to break it up. I caught the collie by the scruff of his neck and lifted him off the beagle. Shamrock saw his big chance to come to the aid of his master—ostensibly—and hurried over and got hold of the collie's tail in his teeth.

Until then I had the big dog fairly well under control. But when Shamrock attacked, the collie flung his head around and got my left forearm in his mouth. Soon I was at the doctor's having my wound treated. I have a white scar there to this day. But Shammy had saved me, to hear *him* tell it, and there we let the matter lie.

Shamrock had the clear and beautiful eyes of the thoroughbred. When you looked deep into them there were flickers of tiny flames coming from somewhere inside. He was not thinking of borrowing a small sum of money from you. He did not want to talk about what a devil he is with the women. His subject for discussion was You, every time and always. Even after an absence of only a few moments, he greeted me as if I had been away for years.

In middle age, Shamrock began to wane a little, and I thought I saw That Look come back to the veterinarian's face. By now Shamrock had survived another serious operation, and one hind leg was off-and-on gimpy. He would be running at full speed and it would throw right out of whack, and down he would go.

But then Shamrock suddenly found his true heaven. One year we took a country place in the mountains. It was close to a primeval gorge where the pine trees stand as tall as the masts of clipper ships, where a stream tumbles for a couple of miles over rocks until it grows into a roaring waterfall and where the ground is springy from centuries of pine needles falling like rain in the nights. There are deer there and bear cubs in the apple trees. Something in that primitive place was balm to Shamrock's soul. He waked me at six every morning, nose nudging urgently and eyes fixed on mine to catch the grand opening, to take him for his walk by the waterfall. I remember him drinking at its edge, then raising his eyes to mine in holy joy.

We took him to the gorge as often as we could, summer and winter. It gave him additional years of life, I think. But still, he was cold at night. He could not jump up on my bed for fear of a fall in the dark with his bad legs. So he slept underneath, wearing one of my polo shirts as a nightgown. The short sleeves made perfect trousers for him.

The end came suddenly.

My wife and I were away for a couple of months on business, and we put Shamrock in a kennel where they knew and loved him and he had the run of the place. But when I went back there yesterday, Shamrock's fires were dim. He could not hear. His eyes were almost sightless. His legs wavered under him. He didn't even know me—until I put my hands around his beat-up little body. Cancer was burning up his insides.

Then he stood up on those hind legs for a last time, put his front paws on my leg and turned his blank eyes up to where he remembered my face would be. The kennel man looked at me and asked the question dumbly he could not bear to put into words. I nodded.

That afternoon I drove Shamrock's body back to the gorge in the hills and buried him there. The bear cubs will tell the others that the little white lion has come home at last.

And when winter comes, the deer will step high in the snowdrifts in that green glade, over the place where lies my little friend, the one I can never forget.

Originally published in December 1968 issue of *Reader's Digest* magazine.

Freedom is not the ability to do what you want. It means the opportunity to soar as high as you possibly can. It means people are not going to judge or block you because of how you look, what language you speak, or where you came from. Use it well.

—CONDOLEEZZA RICE,
Former Secretary of State, in *O*

Little Boy Blue of Chester, Nebraska

by Henry Hurt

He brought an understanding of
life so deep and rare that many believe
it could only have come from God

Frigid winds howled across the Great Plains that Christmas Eve. The deepening freeze quickened the hearts of well-bundled children as the people of Chester, Nebraska, joined Christians around the world to remember God's gift to mankind of his only son.

Around 10 a.m. Charles Kleveland set out for Hebron, a town 10 miles to the north. He took a back road, hoping to spot one of Nebraska's prized ring-necked pheasants. Kleveland eased his truck along the unnamed roadway through vast fields quilted in frost, his eyes scanning the stubble of corn husks.

"A flash of blue caught my eye," Kleveland says. "I stopped and backed up." As his eyes grasped the form, his heart went as cold as the winter wind. "It looked like a child. I couldn't see it clearly for the tall weeds, but I knew that whatever it was, it wasn't alive." Kleveland reached for his two-way radio and told his secretary to ask Thayer County Sheriff Gary Young to meet him.

About 20 minutes later, Sheriff Young and prosecuting attorney Dan Werner stood on the frozen roadway. With the windchill factor ranging to 40 degrees below zero, they looked at the figure lying in waist-high weeds under a dusting of snow. Sheriff Young approached the body. "The boy's eyes were closed, and he was dressed in a light-blue blanket sleeper," says Young. "His left hand was resting on his chest, like he was asleep. I kept hoping it was a doll. Then I saw the hairs on the back of his hand."

The child, about 9 years old, was dead. There, at the edge of a field on this bitter Christmas Eve, the questions came immediately. *Is he ours? Who killed him? Are our people in danger?*

* * *

The Christmas season in Chester had arrived wrapped in tradition and familiarity. Children listened to the story of Christ's birth, keeping a corner of their minds reserved for the gifts they might receive. Their parents, too, tried to focus on the real meaning of Christmas, but the spirit seemed thin. Despite one of the best harvests in memory, farmers had gotten low prices for their crops. People worried about the future. Now Charles Kleveland's terrible discovery accentuated the anxiety.

Within minutes, the news—often whispered so as not to alarm the children—had reached neighboring towns and then beyond Nebraska to Iowa and Kansas as well as Missouri and Wyoming. During this season celebrating the birth of a child, an unknown boy was found abandoned, frozen and dead.

As the news spread, fresh details emerged. The men who found the body suspected that the boy had been strangled. How else could the black marks around his neck be explained? Even more chilling were reports that flesh had been ripped away from his face. During these first hours, people assumed that the boy was one of their own. They pulled their children closer. Some checked the locks on their doors, as well as the ammunition in their weapons.

By late afternoon Sheriff Young established that the little boy was not from a local family, a confusing blessing. As fear began to evaporate, it was replaced by resentment and anger—in some cases a vengeful anger—feeding the belief that someone from the outside had come in to commit this atrocity. People like that did not live in Thayer County.

In the evening, church bells rang through the cold air, calling people to Christmas Eve services. Parents held their children lovingly and protectively. The old hymns were sung through tightened lips.

At the United Methodist Church, Chester's largest, Pastor Jean Samuelson struggled with the confusion facing her congregation. Here they were, celebrating the birth of Jesus Christ, only to have had left on their doorstep the body of a child, abandoned and cloaked in anonymity. Somehow, she said, God was speaking to them. She left them with a promise: "Somewhere in God's eternity, this too will have meaning."

But as families slipped out of the churches into the night, worldly questions remained: *Why was the boy murdered? Who was he? What monster could do this?*

Late that night, husbands and wives quietly wondered about a much deeper question: If God was really a part of every life in Chester, Nebraska— and most believed that he was—then what did he mean by this?

The boy, whom some had come to call Little Boy Blue, had found his final resting spot in the heart of America. Indeed, Chester is only 50 miles from the precise geographic center of the country. The body was discovered only a mile from Highway 81, which stretches from Mexico to Canada, bisecting the United States. Tens of thousands of trucks and cars stream north and south; any one of them could have borne the little boy.

Authorities were optimistic about a speedy resolution. The boy was anything but a waif. He was well developed and properly nourished. His bone development indicated he was around 9 or 10 years old. He weighed about 55 pounds and was about 4 feet, 3 inches tall. His teeth were in excellent condition—not a filling or a cavity. He had sandy hair and light freckles on his face. He was a *cared-for* child—a loved child. Surely, someone, somewhere, was desperately seeking him.

Police were confident that this was a homicide. As soon as the body could be matched with a name, the authorities figured, they could connect him with the people who had left him. Arrests would follow.

But the dark markings on the boy's neck turned out to be freeze burns. Small animals had gnawed away the flesh from his face. It seemed certain the boy was already dead when placed along the road. There was not a hint of trauma or abuse. Despite all the examinations, no cause of death could be determined.

Another puzzle was that the boy's body was so clean, as if it had been washed. His fingernails were clean and neatly clipped. The cuticles of each finger were pushed back. His hair was clean and carefully cut. The bottoms of his feet were free of dirt, suggesting he had been placed in the sleeper after his death, which pathologists calculated took place on December 22.

As the time went by, more than a thousand leads were pursued, including fingerprint checks and comparisons with dental records of missing children. Every major national and international resource was used in trying to identify the boy. Not one solid clue emerged.

Coming piecemeal, these developments nourished a stunning mystery. The number of well-preserved bodies of children this age that are not identified is so small that experts are hard put to find a single similar case. It is equally astonishing for medical experts, under comparable circumstances, not to be able to determine a cause of death. The mystery of Little Boy Blue—his identity as well as the cause of his death—is stupefying in its uniqueness.

Out of all this arose a sad but sure feeling: since no one seems to have ever reported the boy missing, it must have been his loved ones who left him along the roadside. For many in Chester, anger gave way to confusion, which mellowed into compassion.

People had puzzled over why the body was so poorly hidden. Indeed, a nearby culvert would have concealed the body until the spring thaw, maybe forever. Perhaps this child, Little Boy Blue, had died of natural causes and had been left in order to be found.

*   *   *

Three months after Christmas, authorities abandoned hope of easily identifying Chester's little boy. The county prosecutor released the body for burial. During the investigation, people from all over the country sent in contributions to give the child a proper burial.

As things happened, his funeral coincided with the most powerful and mysterious of all Christian observances: Easter. By this time a feeling stirred that, somehow, it seemed appropriate to call the boy Matthew, which means "Gift of God."

Close to 450 people filled the United Methodist Church on March 22, 1986. Pastor Samuelson turned to the 25th chapter of Matthew. In that passage the Lord commends the righteous for having fed him when he was hungry, given him drink when he was thirsty, taken him in when he was a stranger and clothed him when he was naked. In this story, when the people respond that they do not recall having ever done these things, Jesus replies, "I assure you, insofar as you did it unto one of the least of these, you did it unto me."

Jean Samuelson told those gathered that even today Christ speaks to people through the hungry, the sick, the lonely, those who are thirsty and naked. "This little one was a stranger, not clothed for winter, sick. He haunted me. I asked in prayer, 'Lord, why do you keep speaking to me about this child? Why should I feel guilt?'

"The answer: 'He has been in your life in other forms, and you have not heard him or seen him because you were too busy trying to prove yourself worthy.'"

She then told the congregation: "Those who left the little boy were probably once just like him—little children who fell through the cracks of a society that had not yet heard fully Christ's message to a selfish world. They may have been fearful of the law. They may have been confused or ill themselves. God is not asking us to know their hearts. *God is asking us to examine our own.*

"The boy's death and burial connect the two most important days in the Christian calendar, and that would seem to be a special sign to us. It is time we died in our old life and became resurrected to a new life—a life big enough to include one more little brother or sister or friend who has no one to care."

Then Jean Samuelson recalled the night the little boy was left. "I know there were tears by that roadside," she said. "The boy was gently placed on the ground, his hand over his heart. It was as if someone had said, 'I am so sorry, little one. This is the best that I can do for you. Rest now, and go home to God.'"

Jean Samuelson addressed the issue of anger and hate that had been prevalent when the boy was first found. "Christ is saying to us, 'Heed your own heart. Listen to your own words. Watch your own actions. When they are healed, you will see others with new vision, new forgiveness. I call to you from the bed of a cancer patient, from a prison cell. I look at you from the eyes of a starving child. I whisper your name from the body of a small boy left by a country road in rural Nebraska.'"

Then she bowed her head and offered the first prayer taught to millions of Christian children:

Now I lay me down to sleep
I pray the Lord my soul to keep.
If I should die before I wake,
I pray the Lord my soul to take.
—Amen.

Out of the silence that followed there rose the voices of children and grown-ups singing, with no accompaniment, a single verse of "Amazing Grace."

The coffin, donated by a company in Kansas, was taken to the Chester graveyard. The gravedigger refused payment. The vault had also been sent without charge from a company in Kansas. In a plot given by an ill and widowed pensioner, Little Boy Blue was laid to rest in the dark Nebraska soil. The grave was marked with a red granite monument, donated by a company in South Dakota and by the Chester community:

Little Boy
Abandoned
Found Near
Chester, Neb.
December 24, 1985
***
Whom We Have Called
"Matthew"
Which Means "Gift of God"

Through summer and winter, people have kept flowers on the grave. Children leave toys there. The graveyard is along Highway 81, and hundreds of people have pulled off to look at the marker. It is even possible that those who left the boy have been to visit the grave.

People still talk about the little boy, and most hope someday to know the truth about what happened to him. Money that flowed in from around the country has been donated to Hebron's Blue Valley Care Home, where a new room will be named in the boy's memory.

The child is never far from Jean Samuelson's mind. "Great love flowed toward this boy from all of us, and great power flowed back," she says. "It is a power that brings us an understanding about ourselves that is so rare it can only be a gift from God.

"People were moved to examine their hearts. They learned the folly of judging others and making unjustified assumptions. The Lord allowed this boy to come into our community so we could better see ourselves. He was given to us not to stimulate condemnation of others but to help us find meaning in our own lives."

*   *   *

On this Christmas Eve in Chester, bells will ring out through the winter night. Voices will rise in celebration of the birth of a child nearly 20 centuries ago. Prayers will sound for peace on earth and good will among men.

The people of this little town nestled in the very heart of America will also think of another child who came to them at Christmas. That child stirred the eternal lessons of Christ, making them come alive for thousands of people.

"Christmas is a time for hope, for love, for joy," says Jean Samuelson. "We pray that God's love will overcome the fear of those who left their tears by the roadside with that little boy. Should they come forward, they will find the most precious of God's gifts—inner peace, the peace that passes understanding, the peace of Christ."

Originally published in December 1987 issue of *Reader's Digest* magazine.

Humor Hall of Fame

"I performed for the troops in Guantanamo Bay. I signed autographs for people who've been gone from America for so long they didn't realize that I'm not famous."

—MIKE BIRBIGLIA

While serving in Vietnam, my friend was in a mud-filled hole that had been dug into the side of a berm and covered with lumber for protection. The one extravagance: a bare lightbulb hung from the "ceiling." One guy was reading a newspaper article from back home about a congressional investigation into why some troops were living in relative luxury. He put down the paper, turned to my friend and said, "Well, there goes the lightbulb."

—JAMES VALOUCH

After getting my degree in environmental law, I was assigned as chief of environmental law, overseeing a number of Air Force bases. One of the first calls posed a complex legal question and I was completely flummoxed. "Hmm," I said. "I'll find out the Air Force expert in that area and get back to you." After a slight pause, the officer replied, "Well, sir, that would be you."

—DAVID HOARD

"Excellent strategy, General, though I fear the enemy might be full size."

The Doctor of Lennox

by A.J. Cronin

The Most Unforgettable Character I Ever Met

The most unforgettable character I ever met? To my surprise I find myself thinking, not of some famous statesman, soldier or tycoon, but of a simple soul who had no wish to dominate an empire, but set out instead to conquer circumstance—and himself.

I first knew him as a boy, small, insignificant and poor, who hung on to us, so to speak, by the skin of his teeth—barely accepted by the select band of adventurous youths of which I was one in my native Scottish town of Levenford.

If he were in any way remarkable, it was through his defects. He was quite comically lame, one leg being so much shorter than the other that he was obliged to wear a boot with a sole six inches thick. To see him run, saving his bad leg, his undersized form tense and limping, the sweat breaking out on his eager face, well—Chisholm, the minister's son, acknowledged wit of our band, hit the nail on the head when he dubbed him Dot-and-Carry. It was shortened subsequently to Carry. "Look out," someone would shout, "here comes Carry. Let's get away before he tags on to us." And off we would dart, to the swimming pool or the woods, with Carry, dotting along, cheerful and unprotesting, in our wake.

That was his quality, a shy, a smiling cheerfulness—and how we mocked it! To us, Carry was an oddity. His clothes, though carefully patched and mended, were terrible. Socially he was almost beyond the pale. His mother, a gaunt little widow of a drunken loafer, supported herself and her son by scrubbing out sundry shops. Again Chisholm epitomized the jest with his classic epigram, "Carry's mother takes in stairs to wash."

Carry much preferred the open countryside to a stuffy prayer meeting.

Carry supplemented the family income by rising at 5 o'clock every morning to deliver milk. This long milk round sometimes made him late for school. Glancing down the arches of the years, I can still see a small lame boy, hot and trembling, in the middle of the classroom floor, while the master, a sadistic brute, drew titters with his shafts.

"Well, well … can it be possible ye're late again?"

"Y-y-yes, sir."

"And where has your lordship been? Taking breakfast with the provost no doubt?"

"N-n-n-n-"

At such moments of crisis Carry had a stammer which rose and tortured him. He could not articulate another syllable. And the class, reading permission in the master's grim smile, dissolved in roars of mirth.

If Carry had been clever, all might have been well for him. In Scotland everything is forgiven the brilliant "lad o' pairts." But though Carry did well enough at his books, oral examinations were to him the crack of doom.

There was heartburning in this fact for Carry's mother. She longed for her son to excel, and to excel in one especial field. Poor, humble, despised, she nourished in her fiercely religious soul a fervent ambition. She desired to see her son an ordained minister of the Church of Scotland. Sublime folly! But Carry's mother had sworn to achieve the miracle or die!

Carry much preferred the open countryside to a stuffy prayer meeting. He loved the woods and moors and the wild things that lived there—was never happier than when tending some sick or maimed creature picked up on his wanderings. He had a most uncanny knack of healing. In fact, Carry had a tremendous longing to be a doctor.

But obedience was inherent in his gentle nature, and when he left school it was to enter college as a student of divinity. Heaven knows how they managed. His mother scrimped and saved, her figure grew more gaunt, but in her deep-set eye there glowed unquenchable fire. Carry himself, though his heart was not in what he did, worked like a hero.

And so it happened, quicker than might have been imagined, that Carry was duly licensed at the age of 24 in the cure of souls according to the Kirk of Scotland. Locally there was great interest in the prodigy of the scrubwoman's son turned parson. He was proposed for the parish church assistantship and named to preach a trial sermon.

A full congregation assembled to see "what was in the young meenister." And Carry, who for weeks past had rehearsed his sermon, ascended the pulpit feeling himself word-perfect. He began to speak in an earnest voice and for a few moments he went well enough. Then all at once he became conscious of those rows and rows of upturned faces, of his mother dressed in her best in a front pew, her eyes fixed rapturously upon him.

A paralyzing shiver of self-distrust swept over him. He hesitated, lost the thread of his ideas and began to stammer. Once that frightful impotence of speech had gripped him he was lost. He labored on pitifully, but while he struggled for the words he saw the restlessness, the

A strange figure he made, with his shabby suit, his limp and stoop, among the gay young bucks who were his fellow students.

significant smiles; heard even a faint titter. And then again he saw his mother's face, and broke down completely. There was a long and awful pause, then falteringly Carry drew the service to a close by announcing the hymn.

Within the hour, when Carry's mother reached home, she was mercifully taken by an apoplectic seizure. She never spoke again.

The funeral over, Carry disappeared from Levenford. No one knew or cared where he went. He was stigmatized, branded contemptuously for life, a failure. When some years later news reached me that he was teaching in a wretched school in a mining district, I thought of him for a moment, with a kind of shamefaced sorrow, as a despairing soul, a man predestined for disaster. But I soon forgot him.

I was working in Edinburgh when Chisholm, now first assistant to the Regius Professor of Anatomy there, dropped into my rooms one evening. "You'll never guess," he grinned, "who's dissecting in my department. None other than our boyhood friend, Dot-and-Carry."

Carry it was. Carry, at nearly 30 years of age, starting out to be a doctor! A strange figure he made, with his shabby suit, his limp and stoop, among the gay young bucks who were his fellow students. No one ever spoke to him. He occupied a room in a poor district, cooked his own meals, husbanded the slender savings from his teacher's pittance. I saw something of his struggle for the next two years. His age, appearance and traitorous stammer hampered him. But he went plodding indefatigably on, refusing to admit defeat, the old dogged cheerfulness and hopeful courage still in his eyes.

* * *

Time marched on. Five years and more. I found myself in London, and had long since again lost touch with Carry. But I saw much of Chisholm, whose good looks and glib tongue had destined him for political honors. He was now indeed a Member of Parliament and a junior minister into the bargain. In May of 1934 I went with him for a fishing holiday at Lennox in the Highlands. The food at our inn was vile and the landlady a scrawny shrew. It was something of a satisfaction when, two days after our arrival, she slipped on the taproom floor and damaged her kneecap. Perfunctorily, we two renegades from the healing art offered our assistance. But the dame would have none of us. No one would suit but her own village doctor, of whose canny skill and notable achievements she drew an enthusiastic picture that made Chisholm glance at me and smile.

In a flash of recognition he greeted us warmly, and pressed us to come to supper at his home.

An hour later the practitioner arrived, black bag in hand, with all the quick assurance of a busy man. In no time he had silenced the patient with a reassuring word and reduced the dislocation with a sure, deft touch. Only then did he turn toward us.

"My God!" exclaimed Chisholm, under his breath. "Carry!"

Yes, Carry it was. But not the shy, shabby, stammering Carry of old. He had the quietly confident air of a man established and secure. In a flash of recognition he greeted us warmly, and pressed us to come to supper at his home. Meanwhile, he had an urgent case to attend.

It was with an odd expectancy, half excitement and half lingering misgiving, that we entered the village doctor's house that evening. What a shock to find that Carry had a wife! Yet it was so. She welcomed us, fresh and pretty as her own countryside. Since the doctor (she gave the title with a naive reverence) was still engaged in his surgery, she took us upstairs to see the children. Two red-cheeked girls and a little boy, already asleep. Surprise made us mute.

Downstairs, Carry joined us with two other guests. Now, at his own table, he was a man poised and serene, holding his place as host with quiet dignity. His friends, both men of substance, treated him with deference. Less from what he said than what was said by others we gathered the facts. His practice was wide and scattered. His patients were country folk, canny, silent, hard to know. Yet somehow he had won them. Now as he went through a village the women would run to him, babe in arms, to consult him in the roadway. Such times he never bothered about fees. More than enough came his way, and at New Year there was always a string of presents on his doorstep, a brace of ducks, a goose, a clutch of new-laid eggs, in handsome settlement for some quite forgotten service.

But there were other tales—of midnight vigils when in some humble home the battle for a human life was waged: a child, choking with diphtheria, a plowman stricken with pneumonia, a shepherd's wife in painful labor, all to be sustained, comforted, exhorted, brought back haltingly, their hands in his, from the shadows.

The doctor was a force now, permeating the whole countryside, wise and gentle, blending the best of science and nature, unsparing, undemanding, loving this work he had been born to do, conscious of the place that he had won in the affections of the people, a man who had refused defeat and won through to victory at last.

Late that night as we left the doctor's house and trudged through the darkness, silence fell between Chisholm and myself. Then, as with an effort, he declared:

"It looks as though the little man has found himself at last."

Something patronizing in the remark jarred me. I could not resist a quick reply.

"Which would you rather be, Chisholm—yourself, or the doctor of Lennox?"

"Confound you," he muttered. "Don't you know?"

Originally published in September 1939 issue of *Reader's Digest* magazine.

A.J. Cronin's memorable pen portrait of "Dot-and-Carry," butt of boyhood jokes, was the first of the series written by famous authors of America and of Europe for Reader's Digest *on "The Most Unforgettable Character I Ever Met."*

Whether it's beauty
or fashion, there's an
obsession with youth.
But if we're lucky, we're
all going to get old.

—LAUREN HUTTON,
Model in *Byrdie*

"But We're ALIVE!"

by Doris Agee

A brush with death in the terrible might of the sea brings a new awareness of all that's precious in life

As a child growing up by the edge of the sea, I used to wonder about the people who, on a mild summer's day, somehow managed to drown. I'd wonder how anyone could be frightened enough of the water to panic and sink instead of simply floating until help came. (This was a basic lesson I had learned early.) I'd wonder, too, why people—good and poor swimmers alike—would wander into heavy surf and allow themselves to be pounded into the sand or carried out to sea. Drowning seemed a ridiculous and unnecessary way to die.

On Tuesday, September 20, 1966, I learned that there is no special trick to drowning. Anyone can do it. Even a strong swimmer like myself, with years of ocean experience, can do it. On that afternoon, at 4:34, I came within a breath of it. Rust has fixed the hands of my watch at that time. My watch cannot be repaired, and I wouldn't want it to be. I want to remember that day.

There were three of us. Don Horan and Jess Paley, from a television-production firm in New York City, had flown out to California that morning to scout locations for a film they were planning. Through a mutual friend, I had offered to show them some beaches near my home in San Mateo. Although we had only just met, we soon drifted into an easy, relaxed relationship. Our spirits were high when, a little after 4 o'clock, we found the beach that seemed perfect for the film.

Sunlight blazed on the rolling surf. There were no swimmers, and only a few people sat along the wide expanse of pink-gold sand. Gulls swooped and settled along the ocean's edge. Just offshore stood an impressive mass of black rocks, and occasionally a wave would hit the base of these and send up a tower of foam. If I'd been thinking, and not simply enjoying the scene, I would have recognized the unmistakable signs of high tide. I missed them all.

Again there was the helpless turning and twisting, the gasping for air, the weight at my legs.

We parked the car near the base of a large, flat-topped cliff whose appearance intrigued us: its chocolate-brown sides soared straight up from the shore, and its wide, flat face was squared off to the sea. We decided to walk along the front of it and see what lay beyond.

Laughing at how ridiculous we looked in our street clothes, we moved in single file across the wet sand. Some 30 feet separated the base of the cliff from the edge of the sea; enough, we thought—or did we think?—for walking. Suddenly, Jess, ahead of us, stopped to remove his shoes, and I noticed with a rushing sense of danger that the rocks were wet to a point well above his head. I was just about to mention it when time ran out.

We all saw the big wave foaming toward us at the same time. There was no place to run, so we drew back against the rock. Instinctively, to cut resistance, I turned my body sideways.

The wave caught me with unbelievable force as it went under me, rode straight up the rock and fell back on itself. Suddenly I was being turned and twisted and thrown down again and again. Within moments I was far out in deep water. Other waves added to the rolling, boiling turmoil. I felt the stinging salt of the water as it entered my nose and throat. Something heavy–kelp?—wrapped around my legs and feet, pulling me down. I tried to kick away the dragging weight, but it stayed with me, tormenting me.

Occasionally my head would break through to the surface and, for a brief moment, I could breathe. Once I came up facing the cliff and saw that it was a long way off. In the ever-changing turbulence I couldn't swim; the best I could manage was an attempt to tread water, to conserve my strength and keep my head above the waves. I concentrated on relaxing, hoping that new waves would push me toward shore.

Then I looked up and saw a huge wave rising, and felt the outward dragging and lowering of the water that always precedes such waves. In the next instant I was being shoved ahead of the wave as it sped toward shore. Surely I would be dashed to pieces against the cliff!

Mercifully, the wave took me only to a point just short of the beach. Don was standing in the surf close by. His hand reached toward me. I wanted to shout, "Don't! You'll be pulled out too!" But there was no need, for I felt myself moving, with incredible swiftness, back into deep water. The wave that had carried me almost to safety was now removing me from it with its backwash. I lost sight of Don.

Again there was the helpless turning and twisting, the gasping for air, the weight at my legs. Once more I was delivered nearly to the beach, and snatched away. It came to me, with shocking clarity, that I was hopelessly trapped. I couldn't get out of the breakers—either onto the beach or into the relative calm beyond the surf. I was going to die.

I saw my handbag floating over a wave and thought, "If I could only catch it when it comes this way." Then I realized that I had no further need of it. I thought of my husband, Bill, and of how much I loved him. When had I last told him so? Who would meet his 6-o'clock train? When would he know what had become of me?

I heard waves crashing behind me, and knew that within moments I would be swept into the sea for the final time.

All thought was halted by an enormous wave that broke directly over my head. I recall little else. Once I heard someone shout, "Hold on! I've got you!" But it sounded faraway and strange, and I felt no hand on mine. (The wave had brought me directly to Don, he told me afterward. He clutched my hand, but it was completely lifeless and slipped from his as the surf tore me back into deep water. He thought I was dead.)

Suddenly, incredibly, I found myself facedown on the beach, half in and half out of the water. Someone called, "Run! There's time!" Don crawled to me, grabbed my hand and fell to the sand at my side. I tried to get up, but couldn't even raise my head. I heard waves crashing behind me, and knew that within moments I would be swept into the sea for the final time. All my will, all my hope, went into the effort to rise from the sand. But I could not move.

Then Jess was there, a shadowy figure over us. Somehow he got Don to his feet and the two of them managed to pull me up. Stumbling, falling, crawling, we fought to get beyond the rocks. It was a slow-motion nightmare, an eternity before we fell in a sodden heap onto the safe, dry sand. We stayed that way for a long time, holding silently to one another, unwilling and unable to let go.

Then we were all talking at once, with breath we couldn't spare, saying foolish, obvious things. We counted our losses—my handbag, Don's wallet. It was too soon to state the truth: we'd been careless, had suffered for it, and only a miracle had put the three of us back on the beach. Yes, we counted what we'd lost—and each account invariably ended with, "But we're *alive!*"

People, many of them now, were standing over us. We were told that we had been carried far out. One man said, "Only a fool would go in front of that cliff at high tide." High tide! I, raised at the edge of the ocean, had not even noticed. Another man said, "I live over in that cottage. I've seen a lot of people caught where you were. Most of 'em don't make it back, even after they're dead."

Finally we were able to stand, and compare experiences. Don had been thrown against the rock by the first wave, hitting his head. He had been carried into the breakers twice. Jess, luckily, had been pulled in only once, and so it was his greater strength that eventually had drawn us to safety. My sturdy wool suit testified to the might of the ocean and the action of the sand: it was riddled with holes, the hem torn and hanging nearly to my ankles.

For several days afterward, I slept very little. My body was bruised and aching, my mind restless. I thought, again and again, of how it had begun: the foolish way we walked in there, leaving ourselves no avenue of escape. I thought of the many times in my life when, with no fear of the ocean's power, I had put myself in equal jeopardy and not been caught. Those days are over. In the future I will swim—and live—with new respect for the forces of nature.

Since that Tuesday, many wonderful things have come to me. I have seen, with my eyes and my spirit, sunsets such as I've never seen before. I have heard a Chopin étude played by a 15-year-old genius. I have burned my tongue with steaming black coffee. I have heard people talking and laughing. I have watched the long grasses bend in the wind, a hummingbird hover, a tear on a baby's cheek. I have looked into my husband's eyes and told him of my love for him, and his eyes have returned that love.

And always I realize that in one careless moment I nearly gave up all these things. Because I came so close to losing them, I can never again take them for granted.

Originally published in June 1967 issue of *Reader's Digest* magazine.

CLEAR A PATH TO THE DOOR

My grandmother told me to "clear a path to the door every night before bed." It makes for a smooth escape if there's ever a fire in the night. But "clearing a path to the door" came, in time, to mean so much more. I learned I'll be much happier tomorrow if I tidy all the clutter tonight. And it's a good habit when getting involved with new people or activities. Trying mountain climbing or whitewater rafting becomes possible when I know I have a safe exit plan if it becomes too risky. That "clear path" is always a wise plan.

—Glynda Hamilton, *Vancouver, WA*

KNOW WHEN TO GO

I was on a four-day float trip down the Colorado River with a large, fun group. At the end, when I said I didn't want to get off the river, another woman said to me, "It's always best to leave while you're still having fun." It changed my outlook that day, and I've applied it to many other circumstances since.

—Maren Hirschi, *Cedar City, UT*

Three Days of Silence That Saved a Life

by J. Campbell Bruce

How a voluntary news blackout, unprecedented in American journalism, enabled police to solve a sensational San Francisco kidnapping case

At the San Francisco *Chronicle* that Saturday afternoon, January 16, 1954, we were in the lull between editions. The day city editor leaned back, his feet on the desk. Two reporters played chess, with kibitzers. I waited for the nod to go home.

Then a phone rang. The editor reached lazily over: "City desk." He listened, scribbled on a pad—then his feet hit the floor. "We've got a kidnapping!" he shouted. The place came alive in seconds. Soon I was pounding out a bulletin for an extra:

> Leonard Moskovitz, 36-year-old Realtor, was kidnapped shortly before noon. A ransom note demanding $500,000 reached the home of his father, Maurice Moskovitz, prominent civic leader, 2900 Lake Street, by special delivery. The note said he was being held by five men.

No *Chronicle* subscriber read that bulletin. Nor, for three incredible days, was the public even aware that a sensational kidnap case was in progress. Before our presses could roll with the extra, Capt. James English, chief of police inspectors, had called our city desk and every news agency in the city. "Call off your men," he entreated. "A man's life is at stake!" The ransom note, he explained, warned that Leonard Moskovitz would be killed if the police or press were notified.

How that voluntary news blackout held became the most amazing story I have handled in a quarter century of newspapering.

The Moskovitz brothers, Leonard and Alfred, were familiar figures in San Francisco. Identical twins, just 5 feet 2 inches tall, they lived in adjacent identical houses in Burlingame, 10 miles down the Peninsula, and their San Francisco realty office was called The Twins.

Leonard had left the office at 11 that Saturday morning, telling his father, their business associate, that he was going to see a Mr. Lund. He had another appointment at 1 p.m. Around 1:30 this second client called to inquire what had happened to Leonard. His father worried for an hour or two, then called the police. At 5:30 Leonard's mother phoned the real-estate office: she had just received a special delivery ... *some men were holding Lennie ... they wanted $500,000 ...*

At police headquarters a routine kidnap bulletin was prepared. But when Captain English, who was off duty, heard the ransom note's contents, he roared, "Cancel that bulletin. We've got to keep this quiet."

"The *Chronicle's* already on it."

That was when English talked to Abe Mellinkoff, our city editor. Mellinkoff agreed that the *Chronicle* would hold off—on condition that every other news outlet pledged to do likewise. There are 21 radio and seven TV stations in the Bay area, three news services, five major newspapers and a dozen small dailies. English managed to contact them all that night and exact a promise from each to cooperate. The *Chronicle's* extra was dismantled, and all media in the area embarked on a voluntary pact of silence unprecedented in American journalism.

Captain English promised to keep the press fully informed on every development. "I'm really sticking my neck out," he said. "But I have faith in the press." To avoid suspect activity around the Hall of Justice, he set up kidnap headquarters in his own home that night; one room was given over to the press. There the father, twin Alfred and intimate friends were questioned, with reporters as silent witnesses. The elder Moskovitz, aghast at sight of the press, protested, "But the ransom note …"

"It's all right," English reassured him. "We have an agreement. Tell the boys anything they want to know." Moskovitz did.

Under the cover of a storm, which luckily raged that night, inspectors set up a radio transmitter in the family home at 2900 Lake Street, in Seacliff, overlooking the Golden Gate. Similar transmitters, tuned to walkie-talkie frequency, were installed in the twins' homes, and a secret radio wavelength was activated at headquarters for prowl cars.

At the *Chronicle* we had saved the type on our bulletin—just in case there should be a leak. We had to stay constantly on top of the story. I fattened the bulletin with the ransom note, relayed from English's home. In Lennie's own hand on cheap ruled paper, it read:

"Dear Dad—I am being held prisoner by five men and they want $100,000 each. Get it for them right away or you won't see me again. *Do not let the police know or they will kill me if it comes out in the newspaper.* As soon as the money is ready put an ad in the *Examiner* personal column: 'L. Ready to conclude sale. Please advise when and where to deliver.' They want $100,000 in 20's, $200,000 in 50's, $200,000 in 100's. All bills must be old. They must not be marked and not in sequence …"

I drove across the Bay Bridge to my Berkeley home late that stormy night with a strange uneasiness at leaving a story written but untold.

Sunday was a day of developing mystery. That afternoon, with the number of newsmen on the story multiplying hourly, Captain English was forced to move his headquarters to the Hall of Justice, where a special press room could be set up. But for once, on a major story, no free-ranging reporters were poking around in search of angles.

English assigned 100 picked officers to the case. The rest of the

1,800-man police force were unaware of the kidnapping. Even the men pounding beats had no inkling of the crime as they canvassed their districts that Sunday with photos of Lennie Moskovitz. All they knew was that this man was "wanted." Others checked garages and parking lots for Lennie's car. They found it in Union Square Garage in the heart of San Francisco. The timecard was stamped 12:31 p.m., an hour and a half after Lennie had left his realty office. In the middle of the night police towed the car to headquarters where they scoured it for fingerprints. It produced nothing.

Only a half dozen of our printers and a dozen of our 120-man editorial staff knew.

They returned the car as stealthily to the garage and an officer took up duty to nab any claimant.

That afternoon I wrote a complete new story for the *Chronicle's* first edition on Monday. A rewrite man hammered out "sidebar" stories: a biographical sketch, the mechanics of the news blackout, a chronology of historic kidnap cases. Two full pages, complete with photos, were stereotyped into plates and hidden near the press under a pile of rags. We were all ready for a big splash; all that was needed was a bulletin on the capture. Only a half dozen of our printers and a dozen of our 120-man editorial staff knew. Similar precautions were being taken in other news plants all over the city.

On outer Lake Street that day a Sabbath calm prevailed. No sign of untoward activity distinguished No. 2900 from its neighbors. Inside, inspectors manned their post. Throughout the area plainclothesmen with walkie-talkies cruised unobtrusively in private cars. Then, in the early evening, a brief flurry occurred: inspectors at 2900 Lake were alerted: "A U.S. mail truck is entering the block. It's stopping out front. The driver is getting out. He's going up the walk." The inspectors waited, ready to pounce if the driver proved to be in disguise. But he merely handed over another special delivery letter. It was the second ransom note, also in Lennie's handwriting. Minutes after its delivery, our reporter at the Hall was dictating the contents to me:

"Dear Dad—It's Sunday morning and I'm still alive but please hurry …
Remember please they know all the tricks and have assured me that

if we play square with them they will let me go unharmed, but if you tell the police before the money is in their hands or try in any way to trap them they will kill me. Nothing has yet been reported in the newspapers for which I thank God."

Down at the Hall, English thought hard. As a lure, and a delaying tactic, he dictated this personal ad for the Monday *Examiner*: "L. Unable to raise sale price. Wish to negotiate. Please contact us." He needed a telephone contact—phone calls can be traced. "It's a big chance," he said, "but we've got to take it." Doug Hayden, chief special agent for the telephone company, worked out an elaborate detection system. In each of the exchanges serving the three Moskovitz homes and the realty office, a bell was hooked up to ring at a call to any of those numbers. Twenty technicians, on round-the-clock duty, traced every call and immediately notified Hayden, now constantly at English's side.

Monday forenoon the suspense of the blackout grew suddenly taut. The New York *Herald Tribune*, on an anonymous tip of a kidnapping "somewhere in California," telephoned its San Francisco part-time correspondent, Jack Foisie, a *Chronicle* staff man. "A kidnapping out here?" he replied. "Hold the line." He checked with Mellinkoff and answered, almost whispering, "It's true, but the papers here are pledged to secrecy. A man's life is at stake."

Several hours later a major New York radio network picked up the rumor and called its San Francisco outlet. "You can't keep a thing like that quiet—we're going to put it on the air," the network representative argued. Frantic, the local station manager had English call New York at once. "If you break the story and this man is murdered," English said, "you will be held personally responsible. Not by the police. The press here has a stake in this—they will hold you responsible." Tempers became increasingly edgy. Would some other paper or station, less scrupulous, smash the story?

What was happening to the kidnapped man during these tense hours? From details pieced together afterward we learned that he had met Mr. Lund at City Hall that Saturday morning—a suave, husky gentleman who had called at the realty office earlier in the week. Lund asked

Lennie to drive him to meet a moneyed brother-in-law and the amiable Realtor obliged. They stopped at a small house in a modest neighborhood. "I'll wait out here," Lennie said, but Mr. Lund urged him to "come on in." Once they stepped inside Mr. Lund's smiling mask dropped. He shoved Lennie sprawling onto a sofa and another man appeared, flourishing a knife.

Mr. Lund, as it later developed, was Harold Jackson, 57. His confederate was Joseph Lear, 43, equally husky. There were only two men, not five. Both had once been private detectives, wise to the ways of the police—and the press.

Lear held the knife blade at Lennie's throat: "One peep out of you and you'll be dead." Jackson fettered his ankles and wrists with chains. From that moment on Lennie lived a diabolical nightmare. He lay on a bed, shackled, blindfolded, ears stuffed, mouth taped. At mealtime they chained him to a table; one of the men always accompanied him to the bathroom. Jackson dictated the ransom notes, leaning over Lennie's shoulder, watching as he formed every letter.

The kidnappers spun the radio dial constantly for news and made periodic trips for the papers. After each newscast and newspaper edition Jackson would sneer at Lennie: "Damn lucky your old man's playin' ball with us." He would slide a finger across his throat, while Lear ominously snipped paper with his keen-bladed knife. Lennie was scared. Was his father really playing ball? He felt sure, once they got the ransom, they would kill him anyway. The more depressed he became, the more confident his kidnappers grew.

Jackson had been dead set against a telephone contact: "That's how they always pick you up." Not Lear: "How can the wires be tapped? The police know nothing." The continued absence of news bolstered their confidence. And after they read English's ad in the morning *Examiner*, they decided to take a chance. At 12:25 p.m. on Monday Lear phoned twin Alfred at the realty firm, using Alfred's nickname.

"Hello, Ollie. How much can you raise by midnight tomorrow?" Alfred tried to stall, but Lear was too cagey: "Get $300,000. You will receive delivery instructions this evening. Run that original ad in the *Examiner*. No tricks.

The kid's sick. We want to get rid of him." He hung up. The call was too brief to trace.

English now summoned Lennie's father to the Palace of the Legion of Honor, an art gallery near Lands End. "Make sure you're not followed," he said. Already assembled were Maurice Moskovitz's closest friends— his doctor, a judge, the sheriff, a bail bond broker. No other cars were present. A drizzly fog shrouded the statuary in the parking circle. It was no day for tourists.

Moskovitz drove up. English slipped in beside him. "About the ransom— I've talked to the others. We are all agreed on a dummy drop." Anguish sharpened the age lines in Moskovitz's ruddy face. A father's love beat back the logic: "No. If something happens to my boy because I didn't follow instructions …"

English became stern. "Maury, if they get their hands on that money, you will never see Lennie again. Who could identify them? Who could testify against them? Only Lennie. *They will have to get rid of him.*" But Moskovitz was too frightened to take a chance. "Please," he begged, "no phony drop."

So the doctor, judge, sheriff and bail bondsman drove to the Bank of America with Maurice Moskovitz and forthwith pooled their assets, even mortgaging their homes to raise the $300,000. Kindly bankers, sensing the urgency, readily initialed loans, and tellers—without knowing why— started at once the long job of sorting and counting the old bills specified for the ransom.

The third ransom note—most alarming yet—was waiting when Moskovitz got home: "Please, for God's sake, don't try to bargain. I swear to God they mean business. They say they will castrate me if there is any further stalling. Please, Dad, do what they want or they will send my vital parts to show the whole deal is over and I am dead."

I felt a chill as I heard this from our man at the Hall. I prayed the black-out would hold.

English called a huddle. Sweat glistened on his bald head as he ordered the specified ad into the *Examiner*: "L. Ready to conclude sale. Please advise when and where to deliver." He then alerted Hayden that the kidnappers would certainly contact twin Alfred again sometime that night. Hayden in turn alerted all chief phone operators. Alfred's home number—DIamond 4-8020—was Scotch-taped on switchboards at eye level throughout the area. "If a call is made to that number, stall—trace it—notify me at once," Hayden said, then added: "This is probably the most important call you will ever handle. *Do not let me down.*"

Newspaper nerves tightened. Would the secret, so well kept for almost three days now, hold? Slips occur in the best-laid plans—and some newsmen are as gabby as other people. Early that Monday evening an Oakland reporter telephoned his father in Salt Lake City to wish him a happy birthday and mentioned that the San Francisco papers were sitting on a big kidnap yarn. His father, a newspaper publisher, failed to understand that the message was confidential and phoned his managing editor for details. The surprised editor asked the AP to check. Its query to San Francisco appeared on AP teletypes in newspaper offices along the way: "We have report of $500,000 kidnapping in SF. Anything to it?" The San Francisco AP bureau manager hit the phone, explained to Salt Lake the need for leakproof secrecy. It was impossible to reach all those who might have seen the inquiry; we could only hope they would let it pass.

Not long afterward a similar query came through from Los Angeles on the United Press teletype—and had to be squashed. The tension was becoming intolerable. A moderate smoker, I was consuming cigarettes by the pack.

Miss Moon's cord was still plugged in. She rang back. Amazingly, Lear answered.

It was after 1 a.m. when I got home. Around 4 my phone rang. It was Mellinkoff: "There's a break—get over here fast!"

The Bay Bridge, creeping with traffic by day, was all mine at that hour. I made the 12 miles to the office in as many minutes. The *Chronicle* local room was cold, cheerless. Regular editions had gone to press hours ago. Only eight of us had been called in. The reporter at the Hall rattled off flash facts. I wrote a fast paragraph to lead the long-held story for the first extra. Then more facts:

Shortly before 1 a.m.—now Tuesday—Lear had called Alfred

Moskovitz's home and put Lennie on the phone. Alfred stalled for time. "What do you think of when I say one, two, three, four, five?" he asked. "Why, that's the date we both got out of the Air Force," Lennie replied— "December 3, '45." Lear, nervous, broke the connection. But thanks to Hayden's efforts the call could be traced to the Sunset district. At once English deployed prowl cars to that area.

At 2:45 a.m. a light flashed on Claire Moon's board in one of the district telephone offices. She plugged in and said, "Operator," then stared fascinated at the Scotch-taped number in front of her. "It's that Diamond number!" she whispered to the chief operator, clamping her hand over the mouthpiece. Then, while the chief operator alerted Hayden and tracers went to work, Miss Moon asked, "What number are you calling from, please?" Then, stalling again: "I'm sorry. What number did you say, please?" Then she put through the call. It was Lear. He instructed Alfred on the ransom drop: Ocean Beach near the old windmill, Golden Gate Park, 8 a.m. When Alfred asked about his brother, Lear hung up.

"Get him back—quick!" shouted the chief operator, hoping to gain time.

Miss Moon's cord was still plugged in. She rang back. Amazingly, Lear answered. "One moment, please, for overcharges." Abruptly she heard scuffling, then an urgent voice came on: "This is the police. Get me headquarters!"

Miss Moon's delaying action had paid off. Inspectors Al Nelder and George Murray, cruising the Sunset district, had chanced to spot Lear's shadowy figure in an outdoor curbside booth. Why Lear stopped to answer the phone no one knows, unless he was one of those people who automatically answer a phone ring. But that was all the time the police needed to nab him.

Nelder realized that any delay in Lear's return to the kidnap house would arouse suspicion—and mean curtains for Lennie. When Lear refused to talk, Nelder put it to him cold: "It's bad enough now. But if this turns into a murder rap, it's the gas chamber." Lear talked.

Nelder radioed English, who arranged a rendezvous a block from the hideout. Three carloads converged on the spot. Approaching the house on foot, in the cemetery stillness of the hour, they sounded like an army on the march. English called a halt, whispered hoarsely: "Take off your shoes—all but Lear!" As they surrounded the house, Lear's footsteps echoed on the porch. Nelder, gun drawn, crouched low at his back. Lear rapped the code knock. Jackson opened the door. Nelder kicked it wide, jabbed the pistol in Jackson's ribs …

My heart sang as I wrapped up the story for our morning extra: "San Francisco's biggest kidnap case—a tightly guarded secret for three days—broke wide open early today …" Soon the news was flashing across the nation in newspaper headlines, radio, TV. It was to be followed later by a report of swift justice for the kidnappers: life imprisonment for Lear, and for Jackson the death penalty, subsequently commuted to life.

Meanwhile, at the jubilant pre-dawn reunion with his son at the Hall of Justice that Tuesday morning, white-haired Maurice Moskovitz exclaimed through unabashed tears: "I love all you wonderful people— the police—the press!" Said Captain English: "This was true freedom of the press—the freedom to withhold news."

Originally published in August 1957 issue of *Reader's Digest* magazine.

Just as trees grow flowers and fruits, humanity creates works of art: the Golden Gate Bridge, the *White Album*, *Guernica*, Hagia Sophia, the Sphinx, the space shuttle, the autobahn, "Clair de Lune," the Colosseum in Rome, the Phillips screwdriver, the iPad, the Philadelphia cheesesteak.

—RICK RUBIN,
Music Producer in the book *The Creative Act*

Dunes and More Dunes

This is the world's largest gypsum dune field. Located in the vast Tularosa Basin, where the weather is almost always sunny and dry, this is home to a NASA rocket-engine testing facility. It also served as the primary training area for space shuttle pilots, though its emergency landing site was used only once—in 1982, when the space shuttle *Columbia* returned from orbit and was rerouted because of bad weather at Edwards Air Force Base. Where is it?

    A. White Sands National Park, New Mexico

    B. Peterson Space Force Base, Colorado

    C. Sand Mountain, Nevada

    D. Rogers Dry Lake, California

Answer on page 287. Photograph by Vanessa Ragsdale

They Volunteered for Cancer

by Ruth and Edward Brecher

At Ohio Penitentiary, courageous convicts risk cancer in a history-making research project for a potential breakthrough in the struggle to understand this dreaded killer

P risoner Frank J—, bank robber, long-term inmate of the Ohio State Penitentiary in Columbus, and linotype operator for the prison's weekly newspaper, read and then re-read the official notice which had been handed him to set in type: "CANCER RESEARCH VOLUNTEERS WANTED."

Scientists from the Sloan-Kettering Institute in New York City, the notice explained, would soon visit the penitentiary seeking volunteers for a heroic experiment. "The study will consist in the injection of live cancer cells (taken from some person who has a cancer) into both forearms of the volunteer—by needle injection under the skin."

No reward was promised; only the cautiously phrased hope that the study might yield important new facts for science's war against cancer. Prisoners willing to participate were asked to send a "kite" (a written message) to Warden Ralph W. Alvis.

Frank J—rubbed his own arm uneasily. Living cancer cells—there? Then he pondered some more—about cancer, about the people he had known who had died of it. Slowly his shoulders squared. He laid the notice aside and reached for a sheet of coarse yellow kite-paper.

"Dear Warden," he wrote, "I want to be the first to volunteer ..."

Not until his kite was signed, sealed and deposited in the prison mailbox did he return to his keyboard and set the notice in type for page one of the newspaper.

"We had hoped, in our more optimistic moments," says Dr. Chester M. Southam, who supervised the project, "that as many as 25 of the men would have the moral courage to say yes, and the physical courage to go through with it." Yet on June 14, 1956, when Dr. Southam and his associate Dr. Alice Moore reached Columbus Penitentiary for the first of a continuing series of cancer injection trials, not 25 but 130 inmates were waiting expectantly to play their part in the dramatic experiment for medical research.

"I hope I can be of some good to humanity after being no good for so long."

Many Americans will eventually develop cancer. Most cancer research has been focused on the disease itself, its causes and its victims. In the Ohio Penitentiary project, the researchers were standing the traditional question on its head and asking: Why is it that three-fourths of us *don't* get cancer?

"This was no fishing expedition," Sloan-Kettering's director, Dr. C.P. Rhoads, points out. Much evidence had been assembled to suggest that laboratory animals, and human beings as well, are equipped with a built-in resistance to cancer. If scientists could pinpoint the ways in which this natural immunity operates, they might be able to devise methods for strengthening it, extending it and even for providing immunity where it is lacking or has broken down. To pursue this theory, the researchers proposed to compare the effects of cancer-cell injections on two groups of volunteers: one group of men and women who could be presumed to lack cancer immunity because they were already suffering from the disease, and the other composed of normal, healthy persons.

Among the patients at the Memorial Center for Cancer and Allied Diseases in New York City—of which Sloan-Kettering is the research arm— there were some who were willing and even eager to volunteer. To date,

17 patients—men and women with advanced incurable cancer and a very short life expectancy—have participated in the injection experiments.

But where could Dr. Rhoads, Dr. Southam and Dr. Moore find *healthy* men willing to stretch out their forearms to the cancer-laden needle? Long-term penitentiary inmates, unlikely to change their location while the project was underway, had a major advantage over other possible volunteers. So the historic appeal for cancer volunteers was addressed to the inmates of the Ohio Penitentiary, which is convenient to Ohio State University laboratories. The university's director of medical research, Dr. Charles A. Doan, cooperated in the study.

Of the 130 men who sent kites to Warden Alvis, 52 were selected for the first injections. In age they ranged from 23 to 57; nine were serving life sentences and the maximum sentences of the remainder averaged nearly 18 years. Nearly half of them were married.

When the experiment was first announced, an East German newspaper screamed, "Atrocity!" A Connecticut scientist protested it as "an impairment of human dignity." But from the prisoners themselves, and from the kites they sent Warden Alvis, we learned the facts.

"My father died with cancer," one wrote, "and I would consider it a special privilege to do something to help. Thank you."

Another declared: "My sister at home has cancer. Doctors have told her she will never be well again. I want to help in any way possible."

A young man serving his ninth penitentiary year told us with quiet dignity: "I'm an orderly here in the prison hospital. I've seen men come in with cancer, I've nursed them as they got sicker, and I've watched them die of it." To volunteer after such experiences required guts of a very special kind.

Several of the men gave a different reason.

"This is a decision I reached after much thought and a good many prayers," one of the murderers wrote. "I hope I can be of some good to humanity after being no good for so long."

Injection day came and the volunteers lined up outside the door of the office assigned Dr. Southam. Many of them admitted they were scared; yet not one man "chickened out." The doctor chatted with each in turn as he sterilized the skin of the forearm, inserted the needle, then pressed the plunger, sending through the skin a few drops of salty water containing some three million living, virulent cancer cells. In all, seven different types of cells were used. The essential characteristics of each type were well known. The question now was what reaction these cells would produce inside normal human beings.

The injections themselves stung only a little, much like any injection. But in a few days many forearms became stiff, sore, inflamed, hot to the touch. At the sites of the injections small, firm lumps appeared; these grew until some were an inch or more in diameter. Dr. Southam worried with the men through two weeks of mounting concern, until the time came to remove one lump from each man for examination under the microscope, a procedure known as biopsy.

"You can imagine our relief," Dr. Southam recalls, "when the biopsies showed beyond any doubt that the lumps and other symptoms were not caused by malignant growths but *arose out of the men's natural defense mechanisms!*"

In each forearm, countless millions of protective white blood cells called leukocytes had mobilized at the site of the injection and attacked the cancer cells. Larger "scavenger" cells called macrophages had joined the battle. Blood serum had seeped into the region, accounting for much of the swelling and other symptoms. In most of the volunteers, these built-in defenses had killed off the invading cancer cells within two weeks. In a few cases victory took longer; but all the cancer cells in all the prisoners were dead in less than a month.

These results were all the more impressive when compared with results from injecting the same seven types of cancer into patients already suffering from the disease. In these patients there was little or no inflammation, little evidence of leukocytes or macrophages rallying to the defense. The lumps which appeared at the site were caused by growing, multiplying cancer cells rather than by immune responses. In only two of the 17 cancer patients did the implanted cells fail to flourish for a considerable period.

"Obviously," Dr. Southam declares, "healthy individuals have some kind of built-in protection against implanted cancer cells which terminal cancer patients seem to lack."

Can some way be found to enhance this natural immunity? To help find the answer, Ohio Penitentiary's volunteers—now increased in number to nearly 70—submitted themselves to a second and then to a third round of cancer injections.

During the second round each of the original volunteers was inoculated with the same type of cancer he had received before. This time his natural defenses rallied even more quickly and all the cancer cells were promptly killed off. For the third round, each prisoner received injections of a different cancer type. The responses were prompter than in the first round, but not as prompt as when the same type was reinjected.

Just what defensive mechanism is it which terminal cancer patients lack? Tests showed that the cancer patients and the penitentiary volunteers both had about equal quantities of leukocytes and macrophages. Other tests indicated that the cancer patients were perfectly able to manufacture antibodies in the usual way. But for some reason the defensive cells were not mobilized to meet the challenge. One by one, possible explanations were checked off with negative results. Then, early in 1957, Dr. Southam journeyed to Western Reserve University in Cleveland carrying blood serum samples for special tests to be made by Dr. Louis Pillemer.

Dr. Pillemer, who died a few months after these tests were run, was the discoverer of properdin, a remarkable substance contained in the blood that seems to be involved in our natural defenses against a number of diseases. Properdin—the name comes from two Latin words meaning "prelude to destruction"—does not by itself attack an invading particle; but under certain complicated circumstances it joins with other blood chemicals to destroy the invader.

Dr. Pillemer's laboratory tested each of Dr. Southam's blood samples, which were labeled only by numbers. Slowly the data accumulated. When Dr. Southam entered the findings on the chart showing each sample's origin, the results nearly jumped off the paper. All the blood samples containing high levels of properdin came from the penitentiary prisoners; all samples showing little or no properdin came from the cancer patients.

Even more remarkable, perhaps, were the differences among individuals within each group. The serum from the two cancer patients in whom the implanted cells failed to flourish showed relatively high properdin levels. Conversely, the Ohio Penitentiary volunteer whose body had taken longest to kill off the cancer cells was the one with the least properdin in his blood serum. "Seldom before," Dr. Southam told us, "had I seen the quantitative results of an experiment marshal themselves so neatly."

He cautions, however, that the low properdin levels could be the *result* of malignancy, rather than a contributing factor. Additional research is underway to illuminate this question. Unfortunately, the supply of purified properdin is extremely limited.

"A number of the projects which we are supporting financially," reports the American Cancer Society, "are aimed at studying the mechanism of resistance to cancer and what can be done to strengthen the immune response."

Meanwhile the men at the penitentiary wait with impatience for the launching of the next round of injections. A long-range experiment, this will no doubt take years, but it will ultimately reveal whether the injections these men receive can protect them against naturally occurring cancer as well as against implanted cells. Sooner or later, at Ohio Penitentiary or somewhere else, the intensive research efforts underway are bound to pay off either in effective weapons against cancer or in effective methods of prevention.

"I hope it happens soon," Warden Alvis told us, "and so do the men behind bars. But from our point of view, this research has already paid off.

"It has provided all our men—the volunteers and the others alike—with a new sense of pride in our common humanity. Equally important, it has helped the public outside our walls to appreciate that prisons, too, house human beings—men who are still able to respond with nobility when confronted with a noble challenge."

Originally published in April 1958 issue of *Reader's Digest* magazine.

Why Do I Look So Familiar?

by Corey Ford

Mr. Ford's double trouble: "I guess other people look more like me than I do"

I don't know why, but I'm always being mistaken for someone else. Total strangers clap me on the shoulder and shout, "Hello, George, you old so-and-so!" Then they back off, stare at me and murmur, "I'm sorry. You're a dead ringer for George."

I have this double trouble everywhere I go. Stewardesses on airplanes invariably put the wrong overcoat in my lap and then apologize, "I thought you were the man sitting next to you." I've been stopping at the same hotel for years, but the desk clerk still calls me Mr. Furbish. Several times the doorman at my own club has asked me to deliver the groceries through the service entrance. Even animals get me mixed up. The other day a friend's terrier tried to bite me in the ankle. "He thinks you're the postman," my friend explained cheerfully. I guess other people look more like me than I do.

I'm never mistaken for anybody impressive. Usually it turns out that I'm the speaking likeness of a distant cousin in Omaha who isn't quite bright, or a carbon copy of a Herbert Leffingwell, of Montclair, New Jersey, who was arrested for embezzling. One thing about my doubles, they certainly get around. Once, as I was escorting a lady to a Hollywood night-club, a strange blonde leveled a forefinger at me and screamed, "Where were you last night, you two-timer?" I'm still trying to explain that one.

Somehow my face doesn't seem to make any lasting impression. I can always spot that blank look when I greet an old acquaintance. "Why, sure, of course, well well well," he beams, pumping my hand while he struggles to place me. "How *are* you, uh?" At college reunions, I've noticed that my classmates drop their gaze to read the name tag on my lapel.

Or say I go into a crowded department store to buy a shirt. I fight my way to the counter, catch the attention of a salesclerk, tell him my shirt size. He takes a shirt from a shelf, brings it over to the counter, then stands scanning the sea of customers' faces in vain. I wave my hand to show him where I am. "Poddon me," he says, eyeing me coldly. "There's someone else ahead of you."

Sometimes my identity gets to be a sort of guessing game. An elderly gentleman seats himself beside me in the club car and confides, "You look very familiar." I've never figured out a good comeback to this, so I sit and look familiar while he studies me from all angles. "I'm sure we've met somewhere before," he persists. "Did you ever live in Schenectady?" I shake my head. "Could it have been at the Reebles' wedding?" he asks. By this time I'm trying as hard as he is, and I counter with a few questions of my own like, "Do you happen to know a Herbert Leffingwell in Montclair?" I spend the rest of the day trying to figure out who I might have been.

I can't even drop into a neighborhood tavern without having some sodden drunk stagger toward me with a joyful cry, "'Sm'ole war buddy!" I try to ignore him, but he fixes me reproachfully with one bleary eye. "Now don' gimme that, bud. 'Cha 'memmer the ole 368th?" I can see the other customers gazing at me in disapproval. Who do I think I am, snubbing an old comrade-in-arms just because he's a little down on his luck? So I buy him a drink, whereupon he puts his arm around me and begins singing "White Christmas." Generally we wind up getting thrown out together.

I'm forever being thanked for something I didn't do. What am I supposed to say, for instance, when a little old lady grasps my hand in both of hers and sobs, "You were so good to help Oscar in his trouble. I'll never forget it." Certain compliments are even harder to take. "Why, you're my favorite author!" a passenger on a bus exclaimed when she learned my name. "When are you going to write another book like *Peyton Place*?"

My counterparts must be a rather seedy lot, judging from such greetings as, "Hi, there, you old lech," or "Hey, shifty, where ya been—up the river again?" There's one alter ego I'd like to encounter, though. The other morning a stranger in a tight fitting black overcoat sidled up to me on the street and whispered in my ear, "St. Regis lobby. Twelve sharp. I'll have the cash." Then he disappeared into the crowd. A diamond smuggler? Russian agent? Eccentric millionaire? By noon my curiosity was so whetted that I hurried over to the St. Regis. There was the man in the black overcoat, waiting impatiently. I planted myself before him. He stared at me without a sign of recognition, scowled at his watch, then strode out the door.

The worst of it is that somehow I feel it's all my fault. The least I can do is to warn people that I'm an impostor. At a recent cocktail party, a stately matron came toward me wearing that familiar "Haven't I seen you somewhere?" smile. I resolved to spare her any embarrassment by declaring myself right off. "Excuse me," I said to her, "but I'm afraid you've got the wrong person." She seemed a trifle taken aback, but not as far aback as I was taken when I found that she was my hostess.

It's getting to be an obsession. Night after night I dream that I'm standing in a hall of mirrors, surrounded by hundreds of images of people who look so much like me that I can't tell which one I am. Lately I've caught myself nodding to my own reflection in the glass, under the impression that I'm someone else walking behind me. Yesterday a man hailed me by name, then took a closer look and shook his head. "I thought for a minute you were Corey Ford," he apologized, "but now I see there isn't the slightest resemblance."

Maybe I *am* someone else, at that.

Originally published in August 1964 issue of *Reader's Digest* magazine.

Humor Hall of Fame

One Saturday the doorbell rang. Two grade-school children, a girl and a boy, stood at my front door. Each held a few pieces of paper and an envelope stapled together. "Hello," said the girl. "We are raising money for a jogathon for Weldon Elementary. Would you like to donate?" "Maybe," I said. "Just where is this money you are collecting going to go?" They answered in unison, "Oh, it goes in this envelope." I smiled and handed each a five-dollar bill.

—GID ADKISSON

After picking up our 4-year-old granddaughter from school, I was trying to get her changed out of her uniform into something casual when my husband started teasing her. All her squirming and screaming with delight wasn't helpful for the task at hand, so I asked my husband, "Why don't you go and make us some tea?" When he left, our granddaughter Claudia looked at me and said, "That should keep him busy."

—ROSE DEMMER

My twins learned some new adjectives at school today and are currently arguing about whether the dinner I cooked is abominable or diabolical.

—@MUMINBITS

"My dog ate my homework but you'll be pleased to know that he gave it five stars online."

"Can you play with me?" my preschooler asked. "Not now," I said. "I have too much work to do around the house." Taking my hand, and with the wisdom of one who has lived many a lifetime, he said, "Mom, I have advice for you. When people tell me to do work, I don't listen to them. Then I don't have work to do. It works for me. You should try it."

—A. CALDWELL

My brother Ryan and our cousin Carl were buddies at age 3. On hot days, they liked playing together in our big antique bathtub. During one long soak, Carl let out a scream, held up his hands and exclaimed, "Somebody's gonna have to iron me!"

—NANCY WILSON

The Phantom of the Woods

by Doris Cheney Whitehouse

A student nurse and a disturbed patient behold what seems a miracle

It was late when I got off duty. I didn't even stop at the nurses' barracks to change my uniform, but went directly out into the woods which surrounded the neuropsychiatric wing of the big Army hospital. The leaves under my feet were thick and dry, and as I waded through them I was aware of the tangy smell of autumn. The keys to Ward 8, worn on a long rope about my waist, jingled as I walked—reminding me that I was a part of the outside world, free to come and go at will. At the moment this seemed to be the one indisputable difference between Anthony Di Nardo (names and identities of persons in this story have been changed) and me.

Tony was a young GI, a victim of combat fatigue. Diagnosis: agitated depression, manic-depressive type. I was a cadet nurse, sound of mind, on loan from a civilian hospital. And yet, that very afternoon, standing together on the sun porch of Ward 8, Tony and I had shared an incredible vision. The thing we had seen was somewhere in these woods. I had to find out what it really was, to prove to him that it was only an illusion, and thereby end its threat to his recovery.

I thought about the day that Tony had been admitted, three months before. I saw him as he was then, bound to a canvas litter, his tousled hair ebony-black against the pillow. I had watched as a medical corpsman removed his straps and led him into a naked room where he was to be confined for seven weeks. Beneath gray pajama sleeves, white bandages encircled both his wrists.

His face was angular and elongated, and in it I saw a quality of tenderness. Something within me had stirred with an answering tenderness, so that during the days that followed I favored him over all the others.

Tony had been evacuated from his post in the South Pacific, where on a certain morning he had removed the double-edged blade from a razor and slashed the arteries in both his wrists. All through the early days of his stay in Ward 8, the pale hands tore at their restraints in a desperate effort to rip apart the sutures which had robbed him of release. For seven weeks he did not speak or even lift his eyes. There was no violence in him—only the burning desire to be allowed to die. This, through constant vigil, we denied him.

And then, in time, the tortured hands relaxed, and the wounds began to heal. Slowly the spirit found its way out of the darkness. I watched him as he moved about the ward, straight and sure. I saw his healing heart expand to include his fellow patients, and saw him ministering to their needs with the wisdom of one who knew the demons that possessed them.

His eyes were fixed on a spot somewhere out in the woods. He was praying softly.

Tony Di Nardo was almost well. Even our skeptical chief nurse, Lt. Barbara Rankin, was forced to concede it. But then, without warning, on this day in late October, a phantom thing had threatened to destroy him.

The day had begun like any other. I reported for duty at 7 a.m. At noon I went to lunch. Lieutenant Rankin was waiting for me in her office when I got back. "You'd better go and have a look at your protégé," she said.

"What's wrong?" I asked.

"Oh, nothing much." Her voice was granite. "He just got a little excited when he saw the Virgin Mary standing in the woods, that's all!"

I turned and ran to Ward 8. I found him kneeling on the floor, his forehead pressed against the wire screening which surrounded the sun porch of the ward. His eyes were fixed on a spot somewhere out in the woods. He was praying softly.

I tried to make my voice sound light, but it came out harsh and shaky. "Whatever are you *doing*, Tony?" I said. "Get up!"

"But you don't understand," Tony said. "I can see the Virgin standing there!" Then he looked up at me, his eyes entreating as though he were struggling with his own reason. "Is there a statue out there?" he asked.

"No, Tony. I know those woods. There's nothing out there. Now, *please*, get up!"

He turned from me and looked out again into the woods. For a long time I stood above him, wishing that I could

I folded my arms against my body underneath my cape, shivering. And then I saw it, just ahead of me.

take the dark head in my hands and soothe away the dreadful danger. But one does not do such a thing, especially when one is a student nurse.

Instead my eyes wandered absently out over the woods, while a dreaded word rose up and pushed against my throat: *hallucination*. Now he must indeed be judged insane.

But as I gazed, my eyes were drawn to something white—and there in the distance among the trees I saw the figure of the Virgin!

I must have cried aloud, because Tony turned his head and looked at me. "Ah, you see her too!"

"Yes, I see her too …"

* * *

The rest of the afternoon passed slowly, but at last I was off duty and free to search for the strange Madonna. I felt relief in the knowledge that I had only to find the logical source of the illusion to prove that Tony was not hallucinating.

It was getting dark and cold. I folded my arms against my body underneath my cape, shivering. And then I saw it, just ahead of me.

A white birch stump, tall and slender, carved by the hand of time and weather into an abstract image of the Madonna. Even at this close range the delicate curve of head and shoulder, the graceful draping of the mantle, were clearly described in the polished stratum of the bark. In those simple lines were all the grace and classic purity ever envisioned by man in his quest for a perfect Madonna.

I rushed back to the ward. Tony was sitting on a wooden bench, staring out into the woods. He spoke without looking up. "Well, did you find what you were looking for?"

Suddenly I was afraid. Tony had pulled himself together and now seemed prepared for a simple answer, logical and conclusive. But I knew that I had stumbled upon something inscrutable, a thing which transcended all logic and all reason. Yet I was afraid that Tony was not well enough to cope with such a mystery. Therefore, I closed my heart against the beauty I had found and whispered, "It was nothing—just a white birch stump. You mustn't think about it any more."

I should have known that it would not end there.

Late in November, Tony was transferred to an open ward where he was free to come and go about the hospital grounds. Seeing him grow stronger day by day, I began to believe that I had been wise in keeping silent about what I had really seen. So I held the lovely secret in my heart, hoarding it— and I suppose there was talk among my friends about how often I walked alone in the barren woods.

It was a week before Christmas. My training period was over and I was being reassigned. I said goodbye to Tony, and learned that he had been given leave to go home for the holidays. Then I went to my room and began to pack. Suddenly I saw that a light snow was falling, just beginning to adhere to the branches of the trees. On an impulse I got my coat and went outside.

The wind was cold on my face and I blinked my eyes against it. My heart was beating very fast and I began to run. And then, within a few yards of my destination, I stopped.

There, on a glistening blanket of snow, clad in a heavy coat of olive drab, a solitary figure knelt, the white flakes falling like weightless feathers on his bare head. He knelt at the feet of the woodland Madonna, which was clothed in a new whiteness, and the falling snow surrounded and enveloped them both.

When he finished his prayer, I did a thing that one does not do when one is a student nurse. I moved to the place where he knelt and stood behind him, taking the dark head in my hands. Lightly I brushed away the snow that had collected in his hair. "You'll catch your death of cold," I said.

He looked up at me and I could see that he had been expecting me.

"Miracles come in many sizes," he said.

Then he stood and turned to face me, smiling. And in his smile were all wisdom and all tenderness—and I knew that he was well.

Originally published in March 1960 issue of *Reader's Digest* magazine. A *Reader's Digest* "First Person Award" winner.

The minute you start seeing your obstacles as things that are made for you, to give you what you need, then life starts to get fun. You start surfing on top of your problems instead of living underneath them.

—ASHTON KUTCHER,
Actor and Investor on *Running Wild with Bear Grylls: The Challenge*

The Case of
the Murdered
Mother-in-Law

by Gerald Moore

The verdict: guilty—with 25 years to life in prison. To the police, it was an open-and-shut case. To Nathaniel Carter's family and friends, it became a crusade for justice.

Slender and smartly dressed, Delisa Durham Carter, 25, made an impressive witness in the courtroom on May 28, 1982. Tearfully and convincingly, she told the rapt jury how, the previous September 15 at about 2:45 p.m., she confronted her estranged husband, Nathaniel Carter, moments before he killed her foster mother in the older woman's home in Queens, New York.

She had been in her basement apartment that day, Delisa said, when she heard her foster mother, Clarice Herndon, scream. Delisa ran upstairs where she saw Nathaniel with a knife. "I grabbed hold of the knife … and I kicked him," she testified. "I was telling my mother to run." Nathaniel cut both of Delisa's hands badly, shoved her aside and went after Mrs. Herndon.

Delisa testified that she ran to the basement to telephone for help.

Nathaniel confronted her with blood on his hands. He said he would kill her if she told anybody what had happened. Then he left.

Rushing upstairs, Delisa found Mrs. Herndon dying beside the front door. She had been stabbed more than 20 times. Screaming, Delisa ran out to seek help.

*   *   *

Incriminating Web. New York City Police Officer Henry Harrison, Jr., was the next prosecution witness. One of the first policemen at the scene, he had found Delisa bleeding and hysterical on Mrs. Herndon's front porch. Delisa insisted she did not know the man who attacked her foster mother, but she gave a detailed description of the assailant.

Three days later Officer Harrison questioned Delisa at the station house and told her that if fingerprints were found on the knife used to kill Mrs. Herndon, and they turned out to be from a person Delisa knew, he would arrest her for withholding evidence. At this point Delisa became "very hysterical," Harrison said, and shortly thereafter identified her estranged husband as the killer.

Prosecutor Jeffrey Granat then called Associate Medical Examiner Manuel Fernando to the stand. Dr. Fernando concluded that the small, plastic-handled pocket knife found at the scene could have produced Mrs. Herndon's fatal injuries. He described the wounds on Delisa's hands as "defensive." (Dr. Fernando hadn't examined the wounds. His testimony was based on reading hospital records about an hour before taking the stand.)

The court-appointed defense attorney, Peter R. Cooperman, asked whether the knife could have become so slippery with blood during the assault that the assailant could have cut his or her own hands. Could Delisa's wounds have been offensive wounds? Absolutely not, according to Dr. Fernando.

*   *   *

Dreadful Dream. The first defense witness was Raphael Blue, a friend of Nathaniel Carter's since childhood. He told the jury that Nathaniel had been with him the day Mrs. Herndon was killed. Blue, a young musician with a master's degree from the University of Iowa, said he picked Nathaniel up at his apartment in Ossining, New York, shortly after 11 a.m. They drove to the State Department of Motor Vehicles in Peekskill, where Carter made an appointment to take a road test. Then they went to a bank.

Around noon, Blue said, he and Carter stopped at the home of Blue's parents in Peekskill to visit with them, an ailing aunt and the nurse caring for her. Blue and Carter then drove to Elmsford, where Blue mailed a letter by Express Mail. He even produced the receipt for his letter, which was marked 2:10 p.m., 35 minutes before Mrs. Herndon was slain more than 30 miles away—through city traffic.

Blue and Carter drove back to Carter's apartment in Ossining, arriving about 2:30 p.m. Mae Jackson, a neighbor of Carter's, saw him there at approximately 2:50 p.m. when she went to his apartment to borrow cigarettes.

Altogether, Carter listed nine people who could attest he was not in Queens on September 15, but his attorney decided only Blue and Jackson would make solid witnesses.

Then Carter testified in his own defense. The 31-year-old former high-school basketball star said essentially the same things Blue had said. He added that he had last seen Mrs. Herndon on April 1, 1981. It wasn't until September 17 that he learned of her death from a friend in Peekskill. The following day, he went to Mrs. Herndon's home to see Delisa and his son. The next day he was arrested.

On June 4, 1982, the jury began deliberations. Despite the fact that no motive for the killing had been established, and only Delisa had positively placed Nathaniel at the scene of the crime, he was found guilty of murder in the second degree.

Carter could hardly believe his ears when Judge John J. Leahy sentenced him to 25 years to life in prison. The whole thing seemed like a dreadful dream.

*　*　*

Call to Action. Marie Parker was angry when she heard Carter sentenced. Her daughter, Cathy, had married Carter in the Queens House of Detention on January 25, 1982, after his divorce from Delisa had become final. Mrs. Parker's sense of the man told her he wasn't a killer. Now, as she watched the bailiff lead Carter away, she was spurred to action.

That evening, back home in Ossining, Mrs. Parker phoned Lt. James Nelson, an old acquaintance on the Peekskill police force. Nelson listened to her story. He knew Carter's family to be good people. He had watched Carter grow up and play basketball in Peekskill. The whole business seemed out of character for him. Nelson said that if he read the court documents, he might understand what had happened.

Cathy had kept a complete file on the case. Her mother told her to take it to Nelson. As he read the file, he saw that the investigation had been superficial. He would not have accepted such police reports from his men in Peekskill. Too many leads had gone unchecked. Witnesses who had seen Carter the day of the murder were not interviewed. Joseph Fife, who had been around Mrs. Herndon's house courting Delisa the night before the murder, was questioned only once by telephone.

Nelson consulted Peekskill Police Commissioner Walter Kirkland, who had retired earlier from the New York City Police Department. "I'll look into this," Kirkland said, after scanning the court records. "But I'll work just as hard to prove Carter guilty as I do to prove him innocent."

Weight of Evidence. Kirkland decided to start his investigation with Nathaniel Carter himself. Secure in his judgment of human nature, he knew Carter could tell him more about the case than anyone else, both by what he said and what he chose not to say. Kirkland made arrangements to interview Carter in prison.

The Peekskill police commissioner was surprised by the man he met. Convicted of a brutal killing, Carter was calm and easy in his manner. There was no sense of hatred or resentment about him. "Did you kill Clarice Herndon?" Kirkland asked bluntly.

"No sir, I did not," Carter replied evenly.

"When I left that day," Kirkland recalls, "I was determined to continue the investigation."

Over the next few weeks, Kirkland called on all the people Carter said he had been with on the day of the murder. Every one of them substantiated Carter's story. Blue had bank and postal receipts and witnesses to support his account of his activities with Carter on September 15. Cathy added that Delisa had been jealous of her and had once threatened her with a knife.

On December 28, 1982, Kirkland wrote to Judge Milton Mollen of the Appellate Division. New York City laws mandate Legal Aid Society representation when an accused person cannot pay for a defense. Murder is excepted from this mandate, unless there is a special court order. Kirkland sought such an order from Judge Mollen.

About 10 days later, Judge Mollen wrote back to say he had given the case to the Legal Aid Society. The case was assigned to Lawrence Halfond, supervising attorney of the criminal defense division of Legal Aid in Queens, and veteran investigator Ettore Perrazzo. They interviewed every person mentioned in police reports and then followed up every lead those people offered. They soon learned that Delisa Carter and Mrs. Herndon had had serious differences around the time of the murder. Neighbors told them that they had quarreled over whether Delisa could bring a man into the house at night. A background investigation turned up several instances when Delisa had become violent and attacked people.

Suddenly the Legal Aid team realized they had two elements missing at Carter's trial: a motive and a person whose past showed a capacity for violence.

*   *   *

Mounting Frustration. But to get Carter out of prison for another trial they had to show that the first trial had been inadequate, or that there was strong evidence indicating Carter could not have committed the crime.

Meanwhile, Carter had been incarcerated at Great Meadow Correctional Facility in Comstock, New York, located nearly 200 miles from Ossining. Cathy managed to visit him every six weeks. She also did research to help the investigation. "All we could do was to keep working and never ever give up hope," she says.

Carter was still dazed by what had happened to him, but he found the strength to deal with prison life. He had a growing faith that the Lord would see him through the ordeal.

In June, Halfond and another Legal Aid attorney, William E. Hellerstein, sent a lengthy memo to the Queens County DA's office and succeeded in persuading them to review the case. Halfond suggested that the DA's investigators talk to Delisa again. He had a hunch that if she had killed her foster mother, she might now be feeling guilty.

On September 16, 1983, Delisa met with the DA's men. At first, she simply repeated her earlier testimony. Then, suddenly, she said, "You know the truth, don't you? Nate didn't do it. A guy named Cunningham did it."

The investigators were stunned. Then Delisa said she had to pick up her son. They accompanied her to the school and waited outside. Delisa went in and left by a back door.

Several days later, detectives tried to question Delisa again. She had spoken to an attorney, however, and now she refused to cooperate. Because the DA's office had taken Delisa before a grand jury to secure Nathaniel's indictment, and because she had not waived her right to immunity prior to her testimony, under New York law she could never be prosecuted for any part she might have played in Mrs. Herndon's death.

As the days dragged on, Halfond grew increasingly frustrated. Delisa had cleared Nathaniel and accused another man, yet Halfond was unable to get Nathaniel released from prison.

Last Chance Gamble. Finally, Halfond began to suspect that Queens District Attorney John J. Santucci was waiting to find the real killer before he had to face the publicity that would certainly surround Carter's release. So Halfond came up with an idea. If a trusted friend of Delisa's, equipped with a hidden tape recorder, could get her to discuss the case, they might learn the truth. He suggested the idea to the DA's investigators.

Joseph Fife, the man who had come home with Delisa the night before Mrs. Herndon was killed, was persuaded to wear a "body wire." On October 5 and 21, 1983, accompanied by two detectives, Fife drove to Harlem, where New York City police had located Delisa. Fife talked with her while detectives listened over the radio. On both occasions they heard her say that the mysterious Anthony Cunningham, not Nathaniel Carter, had committed the murder.

Subsequently, Delisa left New York, and police found her in Bristol, Connecticut, on January 17, 1984. Again she was questioned about the murder.

That same day, Cathy and her mother, Halfond, Perrazzo and Kirkland waited anxiously in the Queens courtroom where a hearing on whether to reopen Carter's case was to take place. Time for the hearing came and passed. Suddenly, Santucci and his aides arrived. "Larry," Santucci whispered to Halfond, "my detectives picked up Delisa. She confessed."

After so many delays and so much worry, Cathy broke into tears. Nathaniel, quiet and composed, was brought into the courtroom and released. He rushed to embrace Cathy. He thanked Kirkland, Halfond and Perrazzo. He hugged Mrs. Parker. After 28 months in prison, the nightmare had finally come to an end.

On January 25, 1984, the same people again gathered in the Queens courtroom to hear the shaking, tearful Delisa confess. She said that she and her foster mother had argued. When Mrs. Herndon "smacked" her, Delisa went to the basement, got the knife and "started stabbing her."

After the hearing, Delisa, immune from prosecution, returned to Bristol. Nathaniel went home with Cathy to begin his life again.

This miscarriage of justice has spurred efforts to change New York State's immunity laws. The governor's office plans to resubmit a bill in early 1985—dubbed by some the Carter Bill—which would exempt from future use in prosecution only the *information* given by a witness during testimony. The witness him- or herself would not be immune.

Originally published in January 1985 issue of *Reader's Digest* magazine.

Nathaniel Carter says he isn't bitter about the experience, although he did decide to take legal action against the City of New York and several of its police officers. "I didn't have money to fight for my freedom," he says, "but I had my faith in God, my family and friends. I always knew it was going to be all right."

The act of reading is extraordinary—whole worlds created out of black squiggles on a white ground.

—JOHN BANVILLE
Novelist, in the *New York Times Book Review*

The Day the Atomic Age Was Born

by Herbert L. Anderson, as told to J.D. Ratcliff

A dramatic eyewitness account of the world's first nuclear chain reaction

Of the events that have changed man's destiny—the invention of the stone ax, the discovery of fire, the drift into the Industrial Revolution—few can be pinpointed in time. But one, possibly the greatest of all, can be timed to the minute. At 3:36 p.m. on Dec. 2, 1942, the world entered the Atomic Age. And I was one of 40-odd witnesses.

The setting was hardly auspicious: a bleak, drafty, dimly lighted squash court under the abandoned and crumbling stadium at the University of Chicago's Stagg Field. There, within a pile of uranium and graphite bricks the size of a small house, neutrons were being born by the billion each second and hurled out at velocities of 18,000 miles a second. Every one that hit the heart of another uranium atom shattered that atom to produce *two* neutrons. Thus, every few minutes, the silent, violent storm was doubling itself in history's first nuclear chain reaction.

We were too awed to speak. The silence was broken only by the staccato rattle of counters keeping track of neutron production. All our advance reasoning indicated that we were safe. Yet we were pushing into territory never before explored. There was at least a chance that the pile would get out of control; that we would be destroyed and a large, thickly settled portion of Chicago would be converted into a radioactive wasteland. Would this, in fact, be doomsday?

*   *   *

To Tickle a Mosquito. Science sometimes moves at a plodding pace. But, with atomic fission, events had moved at breakneck speed. Only four years before, at Kaiser Wilhelm Institute for Chemistry in Berlin, nuclear chemist Otto Hahn and his young assistant, Fritz Strassmann, had bombarded uranium with neutrons from an external source. Afterward, chemical analysis showed that something extraordinary had happened. Barium and other substances not there before had appeared as if from nowhere and were mixed with the uranium! But if the two experimenters thought that they had split the heavy uranium into barium and other lighter elements, they weren't prepared to say so.

Interpretation fell to a former colleague of Hahn's, Lise Meitner, who because of her Jewish blood had fled from Hitler's Germany to Sweden. There, during the Christmas holidays of 1938, she and her nephew, Otto Frisch, discussed Hahn's data. Possibly, their two brilliant minds concluded, these findings weren't so mysterious after all. Their friend Niels Bohr, the great Danish physicist, had visualized the nucleus of an atom as a liquid drop. If bombardment added an extra neutron to the nucleus, it might become unstable, elongate and divide. The electric repulsion between the two new droplets would be enormous. Within days, Frisch was putting these ideas to experimental test and finding them to be accurate.

Any one of the three rods would quench the atomic fire—unless something unforeseen happened.

When each heavy uranium atom split into lighter atoms, there was a fantastic release of power—200 million electron volts! By itself this was not enough to tickle a mosquito, but if multiplied by trillions it meant a power yield in quantities undreamed of before. The world might no longer have to depend on the fossil fuels alone—coal, oil, natural gas—and face an energy famine when they were gone.

Still, big questions remained if power was to be coaxed from the atom. Could you smash an atom with one neutron and get a yield of *two* neutrons that would go along to smash again and produce four, eight and so on? That would be a chain reaction. Moving slowly, such a reaction would produce heat which could be converted into power. If the reaction proceeded fast enough, you would have a behemoth of a bomb.

✳   ✳   ✳

The Pure Stuff. A fear was with all of us. The German pioneers in the field had almost certainly foreseen the possibilities of such a bomb. If the Nazis got it first, other countries would be at their mercy. This was therefore a race we in the United States had to win. We had to find out if a chain reaction was possible.

Most of the work on "The Metallurgical Project" (our code name) would be concentrated at the University of Chicago. Arthur Holly Compton, of that institution, would head it, and refugee scientist Enrico Fermi would be charged with building CP-1—Chicago Pile No. 1. Fermi had arrived in the United States from Italy in January 1939. (He and his wife and children had gone from Rome to Stockholm to receive a Nobel Prize, and kept right on going.)

As we started work on CP-1, we had no blueprint, only question marks. We knew that natural uranium spontaneously emits a few neutrons. But they travel too fast to cause fission—like a fast-moving golf ball that skims over a cup, whereas a slow-moving one would drop in. We had somehow to slow down these neutrons. Graphite seemed to offer the best available means of putting a brake on them. Perhaps some sort of lattice could be arranged—bits of uranium surrounded by graphite? Then neutrons from one bit of uranium would pass through the graphite, slow down, strike into atoms in another bit of uranium and cause fission?

There were catches in the process. Any impurities in the graphite would act as neutron sponges and put out any atomic fire. And there was no graphite as pure as we needed, anywhere—and we'd want it in 100-ton lots. The problem with uranium—which we'd want by the ton—was much the same.

Industry and universities threw themselves with admirable energy into making the absolutely pure stuff, although we couldn't tell them *why* it was so urgent. By the spring of 1942, driblets of uranium metal, uranium oxide and graphite began to arrive. Pile building began (we were to build 30 experimental piles to provide basic data preliminary to the big one).

The work crews—mainly graduate students—had one of the world's dirtier jobs. Hands and faces became smeared with greasy graphite. Heavy graphite bricks were slippery, and our fingers were inevitably caught between them when we turned bricklayers.

*   *   *

"Suicide Squad." On Nov. 7, Fermi indicated that we were ready for the big challenge. Enough graphite, uranium metal and uranium oxide had been accumulated for the big pile. Work was blocked out. Walter Zinn bossed the day shift. They would plane and shape the 40,000 graphite blocks—some of these drilled to contain slugs of uranium metal or uranium oxide. I headed the night shift. We would lay the slippery bricks in exact patterns just as fast as they could be produced.

Preliminary calculations indicated that the most effective shape for our pile would be a sphere 24 feet in diameter. The most active uranium we had—the metal—would be in the center, with the less active oxide farther out. The great sphere began to grow: a layer of graphite, then a layer of graphite bricks containing uranium, and so on.

For safety controls, we relied principally on three wooden rods, each with strips of cadmium metal tacked on it, running through the pile. Cadmium, the best of neutron sponges, would dampen any atomic conflagration. One rod would be controlled electrically. A second, the "zip" rod, had to be pulled out of the pile by rope; release the rope and it would zip in. The third was for fine control, and it would be hand operated to achieve the level of neutron activity wanted. Any one of the three rods would quench the atomic fire—unless something unforeseen happened.

As a final precaution, three men would be stationed atop the wooden scaffolding surrounding the pile—a "suicide squad." They would have great flasks of cadmium solution to quench a runaway reaction. "If things get away from us," Fermi told them, "break the flasks. But watch me, and don't do it until I drop dead. If you do it before, I'll use a sledge hammer on you!"

By the time my shift took over on Dec. 1, we were at the 48th layer, and Fermi had calculated that layer 51 would complete the job. He read what was on my mind. There would

For 17 agonizing minutes the atomic storm raged, growing increasingly violent. The pile was heating up.

be the greatest temptation to pull out the control rods and be the first in the world to observe a chain reaction. "When you have finished layer 51," he directed, "lock those rods in place. Everyone be here at 8 tomorrow morning."

A few hours later, we completed the final layer. Somewhat reluctantly I followed directions, padlocked our 550-ton monster for the night, and went home.

* * *

Inch by Inch. Morning dawned chill and gray, with a dust of snow on the ground. General Eisenhower had launched his North African campaign. The battle for Guadalcanal was in its final victorious phases. Work was already under way on super-secret atomic-bomb plants, on the faith that a chain reaction was possible. If our reactor worked, then it had the potential not only for death, but for ending a nightmarish war and saving millions of lives.

By 8, we had all filed in and taken our places. I was at a control panel to record instrument readings. Zinn was to pull out the zip rod. George Weil manned the all-important hand rod. The suicide squad was at the ready. Observers stood on a small balcony where spectators had formerly watched squash games. The great show was about to begin.

At 9:45, Fermi, speaking in his quiet voice, ordered the electrically controlled rod out. There was a slight whirring of motors, and the clicking of counters could be heard. Neutron activity was rising. Fermi's mild gray eyes were on the pen as it moved upward on a piece of graph paper before leveling off. Hardly aware of the presence of others, he manipulated a slide rule. Everything was going according to plan.

At 10, he ordered Zinn to pull out the zip rod. There was another increase in neutron production—but again nothing massive.

At 10:37, Fermi directed Weil: "Pull the hand rod out to 13 feet." The counter began to roar. Anxious faces looked at the pen sweeping upward. Fermi indicated that it would level off at a certain point, and it did. From time to time he ordered Weil to pull the rod out another few inches. Each time there was an upsurge of neutron activity, our tension rose proportionately—to a point almost unbearable.

Then the spell was broken. "Let's go to lunch," said Fermi. It was like Wellington suggesting a lunch break at the Battle of Waterloo. All rods went back in, and counters fell silent, except for an occasional feeble click. Even at rest the pile produced 100,000 neutrons a second.

* * *

Atomic Storm. At 2, we began again, moving more rapidly this time. At 3, the counters had to be recalibrated—slowed down to dampen the rattle and give meaning to their sounds. Further, the pen was going off the graph paper. At 3:19, Fermi ordered the hand rod withdrawn another foot. He glanced at the graph, consulted his slide rule, then turned to Compton, standing beside him. "The next foot should do it," he said. At 3:36, the hand rod was withdrawn a final foot. And, minutes later, he spoke again: "This time it won't level off. The curve is exponential"—meaning that the activity would go on doubling and redoubling.

For 17 agonizing minutes the atomic storm raged, growing increasingly violent. The pile was heating up. The first chain reaction was under way. In ominous silence mankind was entering a new age. Fission, we knew, would create new radioactive elements—and with the greatest rapidity. Our pile could be safe one moment and deadly shortly afterward. Understandably, worry was written on many faces. Eyes were on radiation meters, which showed that we were rapidly approaching danger levels.

At 3:53 Fermi turned to Zinn. "Zip in," he said. As the rod slipped into the pile, activity diminished rapidly. The great drama was coming to an end. We had made a safe journey into the unknown.

The Day the Atomic Age Was Born

$$*\quad*\quad*$$

If the world is depressed by the fact that two atomic bombs were dropped 32 months later, it might take heart from the enormous benefits that have accrued from fission. Much of medical science has been revolutionized, and the pace of other research quickened.

On that bitter, blustery winter afternoon, history was changed. Possibly it was for the worse. Hopefully, time will prove it was for the better.

Originally published in March 1969 issue of *Reader's Digest* magazine. A *Reader's Digest* "First Person Award" winner.

Herbert L. Anderson had recently earned his doctorate in physics when, at 28, he was selected by the late Enrico Fermi to help construct the first chain-reacting atomic pile. From 1958 to 1963 he was director of the Enrico Fermi Institute at the University of Chicago, where he became professor of physics.

Mrs. Lee's Daffodil Garden

After her husband, T.W. Lee, passed away in 1954 and left behind 816 acres of property, Helen (pronounced HEE-len) Lee bought a boxcar of bulbs from Holland and planted them here. When Helen died in 1984, it was her request that the garden be maintained and open to the public during each new bloom, usually a few weeks in February and March. But some years, it's open for just one day—or not at all. Where is it?

A. Wetumpka, Alabama

B. Hoboken, New Jersey

C. Gladewater, Texas

D. Nederland, Colorado

Answer on page 287. Photograph by Linda Davidson

Wandering in the Alaskan Winter

by Brian Murphy, from the book *81 Days Below Zero*
with Toula Vlahou

It's December in the Arctic Circle, and World War II airman Leon Crane is the lone survivor of a plane crash. He knows that he'll need to be rescued quickly if he's going to live.

It was approaching noon on Dec. 21, 1943, in the Tanana River valley of Alaska, not far from the Arctic Circle, and the five men on the *Iceberg Inez* were preparing to crash. Minutes before, the crew of the B-24 bomber had been testing a modified system on the plane's four propellers when the plane seemed to stall, sending it diving into a roller-coaster plunge. G-forces slammed pilots Leon Crane and Harold Hoskin as they lurched at the controls. Wind screamed over the cockpit glass. The airspeed gauge was redlining. The flight instruments were blinking out. Then something that sounded like a pistol shot came from the tail, followed by cracking noises.

"Open bomb bays!" Crane shouted to the crew chief.

"Bail out!" Hoskin yelled to the other crew members.

The crash alarm bells jangled like a fire drill as Crane yanked off his mittens to secure his chute. And then, before he knew what was happening, he was in a free fall. He felt for the rip cord. The chute poured out. He swayed beneath it and watched the *Iceberg Inez* spin off before it slammed into a mountain slope and erupted in flames. Crane himself thudded into the powdery snow near the banks of a stream, two miles away from his plane, he guessed. The gas on board would keep the wreckage burning for a while, which would be good for a rescue mission. But the fire also meant the supplies on board—sleeping bags, signal flares, a gun and ammunition—were lost, almost certainly along with any other crew members who might have survived the crash.

Still, Crane shouted out for Hoskin and the rest of the men. He listened for any hint of life. Nothing. He was alone.

The sky was already turning dark. Crane took a few stumbling steps and found that the snow covered a jumble of rocks that made walking nearly impossible. There was no chance to reach the crash site before nightfall, nor did he have any idea where he was. And a broken ankle would be a death sentence.

Fortunately, the 23-year-old pilot had a few provisions to keep him warm until help arrived. He had the silk parachute, which he could use as a sleeping bag. His flight suit was intact. He had on three pairs of wool socks under his heavy mukluks. He also had his flight helmet and a pack of matches, as well as a knife. But he didn't have his mittens, which he'd left on board in the rush to prep his chute. Without them, his unprotected fingers could become frostbitten within 10 minutes.

He tucked his hands in his armpits and thought back to the last radio contact with the air base at Ladd Field in Fairbanks. That had been at least an hour before the plane had fallen, which meant the search area would be huge—a radius of about 200 miles from their last known position.

It was minus-60 degrees Fahrenheit. Crane knew he needed to get a fire going or he might not last the night, so he gathered driftwood. His fingers were numb, but he managed to strike a match. The little flame wasn't enough to catch. He tried four matches, but they did nothing except singe his fingertips.

Then he remembered a letter from his father he kept in his parka. Crane fed it into the wood. The fifth match worked, and a fire rose up. He let the fire thaw his fingers before wrapping himself in the chute. He thought about what would happen if rescue never came. *How long,* he wondered, *would it take to die?*

* * *

In the morning, Crane ran through his odds of being saved. The short daylight allowed little time for search planes. And in this climate, the hunt would be measured in days, not weeks, before it was called off. What if a plane never found him? There was water gurgling up through the ice on the stream, but he had no food. And his hands were already developing a pasty white look—the first signs of frostbite.

Crane was convinced that his best chance of survival was to leave the crash area and explore downstream. The water had to eventually drain into something, he reasoned, probably the Yukon River, and there was a chance of finding a trapper riding out the winter. But first he called out for his crewmates once again. When there was no response, he gathered up his parachute and his matches and set off. It took

hours to cover one mile through the waist-deep drifts and ice-coated rocks.

As the sky darkened, Crane picked a patch of level ground by the stream to build a fire. But he had already burned his only kindling, his father's letter, so it took several matches to get flames going. At this rate, he would have only a two-week supply of matches.

By the fire's warmth, he inspected his hands. They were numb, and the color had drained from his fingertips. It was insanity to try to walk farther, he realized. It was wiser to stay in the vicinity of the crash site for a week, after which the air base would probably call off the search. Then he'd start walking again.

Hunger gripped Crane with an angry, clawing need. He had to find something to eat. Walking in deadly cold under these harsh conditions could demand about 6,000 calories a day. A few days of that and he'd simply collapse.

He saw a few red squirrels, one of the few animals that do not migrate or hibernate during the Alaskan winter. Crane broke off a branch, took out his knife, and began to whittle down a point until he had a spear. Then he took aim and threw. The spear flew through the air, wobbly and slow, missing its target by a foot. Next, Crane tried a sneak attack, jabbing at one of the spry animals. He missed, then missed again. Enraged, Crane grabbed rocks and hurled them at the squirrels. "Go to hell!" he yelled.

Beaten, he spent the next three days wrapped in his parachute in a kind of hibernation, climbing out only to drink from the river and feed the fire.

* * *

Although Crane was alone in the wilderness, he'd not been forgotten. The first rescue flight went out of Ladd Field eight hours after the last radio contact with the *Iceberg Inez*. Within two days, more than 20 search missions were launched—all coming up empty. At the base, the crew's bunks and lockers remained untouched for a while. Eventually, though, their personal items were packed up and shipped to the next of kin.

* * *

With no food and fading hope, Crane felt the need to do something. He decided the river was too much of an unknown, so on Dec. 29, eight days after the crash of the *Iceberg Inez*, he began hiking overland in search of civilization. With each step, he had to plow aside snow. Numbness began to spread downward from his knees. Not a single stride landed easily. He stumbled several times, which forced him to pull his hands from the warmth and safety of his pockets to avoid toppling over. At midday, Crane stopped. In two hours,

In two hours, Crane had gone roughly 300 feet. I'm simply marching to my death, he thought.

he had gone all of roughly 300 feet. *I'm simply marching to my death*, he thought. Crane turned around and followed his tracks back to his campsite on the river. The fire was nearly out, but some wood still glowed. He coaxed flames from the spruce and cloaked himself in the parachute for another night.

He left again the next morning, this time trying to walk atop the frozen river. Crane followed the pathway through white hills, telling himself, *Around the next bend, there will be a cabin with a fire and a family who will feed me supper with steaming coffee.* But bend after bend, it was just more river, more hills. And there was something else concerning him. It had started with a few moments of disjointed, meandering thoughts, and a few times over the past few days, he'd found himself in a daze. Crane felt himself slipping, his judgment fraying because of cold, hunger, fatigue and loneliness.

He was naked and losing body heat. He wrung out his clothes and laid them near the fire.

Dusk gave way to darkness, and as he blindly trundled on, a log cabin came into view, half covered with snow. He stumbled over rocks, running and yelling, not caring that his hands were exposed. He cleared away a drift and opened the door.

The place was about 10 feet wide, with a dirt floor and a low ceiling. A wooden bunk stood in the corner. There was a table with burlap sacks on it, tied with twine. His frigid fingers couldn't loosen the knots, so he cut a bag with his knife. Sugar! There was a tin of cocoa, one of dried milk and a box of raisins. Crane stuffed the raisins into his mouth. He lit a fire and filled a frying pan with snow, and soon he was holding a tin cup of hot cocoa in both hands. Then he fell asleep in the bunk.

When he awoke, he made more cocoa. Sated, he filled his pockets with raisins and set off downriver, certain that there must be a village nearby. The river bent to the west, and the valley narrowed. He hiked on, hour after hour. All he saw was more wilderness. Darkness fell, and a half-moon rose in the cloudless sky. The temperature had tumbled down to 40 below, he figured. It was decision time. His hands were too numb to light a match, and he knew he could not ride out the night without a fire. He made the painful choice. There was no village. He had to return to the cabin.

He stumbled back along the river. Icicles hung from his nose. It hurt too much to brush them off. To stop was to perish. He just kept his legs moving. One step. One breath. Dawn came, and still there was no sign of the cabin. The landscape was not familiar—he had paid no attention when he'd headed out the previous morning. It was close to noon—after 30 hours of walking—before Crane saw the cabin again. He staggered through the door and made a fire. Then he wrapped himself inside the silk folds of his parachute and collapsed into the bunk.

*   *   *

Crane spent 48 hours in bed before hunger forced him to his feet. He stepped outside to explore a small shelter he'd noticed earlier. As luck would have it, it held food, clothes, a rifle, ammunition and, most important, a pair of moose-hide mittens. Crane used the next three weeks to regain his strength. But if he was going to make it, he'd need to carry more supplies. So he took two old boards for runners, pulled a window frame from the cabin and nailed a washtub to the frame to make a sled. He packed it with food and gear.

At dawn on Feb. 12, 1944, 53 days since the crash, he said goodbye to the cabin that had saved his life. He looped a rope harness around his chest and hauled the sled over the riverbank and onto the ice.

The going was tough. The harness dug into his chest, and he managed only one mile in the first hour. For four days he hiked on, his world whittled down to the act of a single step, then the next step. At one point, as Crane leaned forward to push through a drift, the ice folded under his feet. He gulped a breath as the surface gave way. The sled halted his fall long enough for him to twist around, grab the rope and haul himself back. He could feel the water leaking through the tops of his mukluks and soaking his body below his waist.

He had to act fast. Crane lumbered toward the bank with the sled in tow. He surged onto the rocky shore and, with trembling hands that could barely strike a match, made a fire.

Crane strung a rope between two trees and draped his tent over it, forming a crude shelter. He pulled off his flight suit, long underwear, mukluks and socks. He was naked and losing body heat. He wrung out his clothes as best he could and laid them near the fire. Then he cowered naked and let the warmth of the fire slow his shivering.

The next day, his clothes dry, Crane was back on the move. A week had passed since he'd left the safety of the cabin. His legs just kept moving, making maybe four miles a day. He came upon another deserted cabin. Then more days of walking. March 7, March 8, March 9 …

On March 10, at first light, Crane stumbled upon a trail and followed it. It led away from the river, then back toward the ice. There, on the other side of the river, was a cabin. Then came barking. The sound of a dog.

"Ho!" Crane yelled. "Anyone there?"

And for the first time in 81 days, someone answered.

*   *   *

A trapper took Crane in, gave him food and clothes, and took him by dogsled to Woodchopper, Alaska, where a mail plane flew him back to Ladd Field. He was the lone survivor of the crash of the *Iceberg Inez*.

Crane met a nurse at Ladd Field. After the war, they got married and had six children. They made their home in the Philadelphia area, where Crane had a career first as an aeronautical engineer and later as a home builder. Leon Crane, who died in 2002 at age 83, rarely spoke of his time in Alaska. Other people had faced far worse in the war, he'd explain. What he experienced was, by comparison, simply a breeze.

Originally published in December/January 2017-2018 issue of *Reader's Digest* magazine.

CURB YOUR APPETITE

"Don't have a champagne appetite on a beer pocketbook."
That was my dad's mantra. He had been well-to-do early in life
but hadn't changed his spending when he wasn't any longer.
Fortunately, I have a beer appetite.

—Mike Fleischmann, *Fort Collins, CO*

MAKE TIME TO DO IT RIGHT

"If you don't have time to do it right the first time, how are you
going to find time to do it over?" Advice from my 91-year-old
dad that I've shared with my daughter and granddaughter.

—Sharon Price, *Mobile, AL*

Humor Hall of Fame

My sister went shopping for jeans with her husband. While he waited outside the fitting room he heard her crying. He said, "Honey, it doesn't matter if you've gone up a size or two." She came out, limping and upset. She'd stubbed her toe.

—JULIE LAW

At a wedding I attended, the groom and groomsmen stood at the altar in anticipation of the bride's arrival. My 3-year-old niece was also filled with anticipation. Pointing to the men, she shouted, "I wonder which one she'll pick?"

—RUTH MUCHEMORE

"Look, I know it's not perfect, but by and large, the jury system has worked very well for our marriage."

> *When my wife and I argue, we're like a band in concert: We start with some new stuff, and then we roll out our greatest hits.*
>
> —COMEDIAN FRANK SKINNER

Married 37 years, my brother- and sister-in-law, Jake and Fran, were chatting with another couple. Jake admired his friend's ornate gold-and-diamond ring and lamented that all he had was a gold washer, indicating his plain gold wedding band. That December a small box appeared under the Christmas tree for Jake. It was an expensive gold-and-diamond ring. Thanking Fran, he added, "You shouldn't have spent so much money." "Oh, I didn't," she replied. "I took it out of your top dresser drawer. It's the ring I gave you for our 25th wedding anniversary."

—V.K. HOEPPNER

While on vacation, an older couple stopped for lunch at a little diner. After they got back on the road and had traveled some distance, the wife realized she'd left her prescription reading glasses behind. Her husband grumbled all the way back to the restaurant, and by the time they got there, she was really feeling terrible for having inconvenienced him. Just as she started getting out of the car, he called to her: "As long as you're going in, you might as well get my wallet. I must have left it by the cash register."

—LENORE CLARK

If you get drunk and want to lie, you're a fiction writer. If you get drunk and tell the truth, you're a memoirist. And if you get drunk and want to lie on the hood of a car and look at the sky, you're a poet.

—REBECCA MAKKAI
Novelist, in an interview with The Center for Fiction

Are You Too Boring for Therapy?

by Cassie Barradas

Six tips for spicing up the relationship

Worried that your dull problems and weak-sauce neuroses are putting your therapist to sleep? Spent yet another tedious session talking about your mother? *Again?*

Don't fear: therapy is about self-improvement. Yes, your counselor is in this field because she wants to make a positive difference in the lives of others, but that doesn't mean you shouldn't make her day positively different. This helpful guide can help you spice up your sessions—and self-actualize in ways neither of you have expected!

Share your interests. She may know nearly everything about your relationships with your family and friends. But does she know about your relationship to the hit 1990s television series *Friends*? While it's true that your therapist pursued her career path to help others navigate life's toughest circumstances, it's also true that an hour spent determining whether you're a Ross or a Phoebe is a valuable psychological exploration that says a lot about both of your capabilities.

*   *   *

Dress for the occasion. Your therapist may have a master's degree in psychology, but you can still wow her with your mastery of fashion. A 9-foot velvet cape makes a powerful statement without you having to use any words at all.

*   *   *

Add some mystery. Even the most professional relationship needs an element of surprise. Yes, it's been wonderful having your therapist help you unpack your emotions every Thursday afternoon. But mixing things up with a Monday session will have her saying, "Did your schedule change?"

You can eagerly reply, "No, it did not. I just thought this would make things more interesting for you," to which she will doubtless respond, "I'm happy to schedule appointments during all available work hours." Exhilarating!

*   *   *

Incorporate surprises. Saying "Thank you for helping me to see my worth" is so boring, and your kind, professional therapist deserves more. Try instead, "I bought a duck farm, but I'm not sure what to name all the ducks." I assure you, she has never heard this line before, and that's a much better thank you.

*　*　*

Change your makeup routine! It's really amazing how your therapist has helped you make boundaries for yourself. You can reflect that by literally drawing a line on one side of your face with a thick black Sharpie and not ever acknowledging it. She probably gets pretty tired of seeing all her other clients' faces without lines drawn on them. This is sure to leave a mark on your face—but also in her heart.

*　*　*

Go on adventures together. So many of your appointments involve talking about the same locations: work, home, your innermost self. While it might be wildly inappropriate to literally travel with your therapist, a bit of emotional sightseeing could be just what you need to keep things fresh. Use mixed metaphors to let her know that "This early bird has bigger fish to fry." The biggest adventure of all will be figuring out what you even meant by that!

Originally published in January/February 2020 *Reader's Digest* international editions.

"There Wasn't Time to Scream"

by Per Ola and Emily D'Aulaire

A story of the horror and heroism that took place one dreadful night in Kansas City—and a warning that it could happen again elsewhere

James McMullin, a jovial trial lawyer, was riding an escalator from a balcony restaurant area to the main floor of Kansas City's Hyatt Regency Hotel. Below him the dazzling atrium lobby was jammed with more than 1,500 people attending the hotel's popular five-to-eight Friday tea dance, a nostalgic throwback to Big Band days. Above the dance floor, revelers had spilled onto the hotel's "skybridges"—elevated, 120-foot-long walkways with waist-high side panels of thick glass that spanned the five-story lobby.

As McMullin stepped off the escalator, the band was playing Duke Ellington's "Satin Doll." A dance contest was in full swing. It was 7:05 p.m., July 17, 1981.

Suddenly, he heard a series of sharp cracks, then a wrenching, screeching noise. Unbelieving, he watched as the fourth-story skybridge split near the center and plunged downward, bearing its human cargo. "It hit the second-story walkway directly beneath it with a *crumph*, and then both

The still intact third skybridge hangs and sections of the two walkways that collapsed lie on the floor.

thundered onto the crowded floor—*crumph, crumph*," he recalls. "There wasn't time to scream. People and tables as far as a hundred feet away were mowed down by flying glass and debris."

As the echoes of the mighty collapse subsided there was an interval of eerie silence. Then moans and cries began rising from beneath heaps of debris as high as six feet. McMullin rushed to the fallen walkways thinking, *My God, we've got to help!* Choking from the plaster dust that filled the air, he and others tried to pry up parts of the fallen skybridges. It was hopeless. Each of the approximately 36-ton walkways had broken into four huge sections now sandwiched tightly together—except for one ominously tilted span that balanced precariously at the second-floor level.

"The carnage was worse than anything I'd ever seen in battle," says McMullin, who served as a Marine officer in World War II and Korea. "Arms, legs and mangled people protruded from under the wreckage. We'd pry and dig, but we couldn't get to them. Men were crying in frustration, including me."

✳   ✳   ✳

"Emergency!" Owned by Hallmark Cards' Crown Center Redevelopment Corporation, the $50-million hotel had been opened a year before, part of a half-billion-dollar revitalization of the downtown area of Hallmark's hometown. The building's dramatic and spacious atrium lobby reflected the unique Regency style that had transformed hotel architecture when it was first adopted by the Hyatt chain in Atlanta in 1967. The architecturally stunning hotel had helped confirm Kansas City's prominence as one of the nation's top 10 convention center locations. And the festive Friday-night tea dances had made the Hyatt one of the town's more popular social hubs for local residents as well.

After the skybridges fell, there was a period of pure disbelief among onlookers in the shattered lobby, and it was a full three minutes before anyone managed to dial the Kansas City Fire Dispatch Office. In a terror--filled voice a front-desk receptionist cried, "Could you please come to the Hyatt Regency! Hyatt Regency! Immediately! Skybridges! Holding people! Fell... crushed ... immediately ... Hyatt Regency!"

Three minutes later the first fire truck rolled onto the scene. Not knowing what to expect, Capt. Joseph Thomas made his way through the revolving front doors and, for a brief moment, stood transfixed at the devastation spread before him. Then he grabbed his portable transceiver and radioed the dispatcher, his voice a scream: "Emergency! Front lobby! We've got people trapped under there. We need heavy equipment to move it, and we need ambulances!"

*   *   *

Sweat, Tears and Blood. Word of the disaster spread rapidly through the city. Construction workers came running from a nearby job where they had been working the evening shift, bringing jackhammers and other equipment with them. As rescue workers pulled out those they could, cabs, private vans and city buses lined up with a helicopter and paramedic ambulances to help evacuate the wounded.

In one sense, the city was extraordinarily prepared to cope with the horrors of this night. Just five months earlier a new disaster plan had been implemented. It had been tested only weeks before in two emergencies involving critical injuries.

Within half an hour of the collapse, the first 200 of what would grow to almost a thousand firemen, police officers, medical personnel, and volunteers from the Red Cross and Salvation Army were there, trying to untangle the dead, dying and living from the nightmarish mess.

Most of the victims caught directly under the bridges never had a chance.

Once the heavier extrication equipment was called in and spotlights were put on, it became stiflingly hot and humid in the atrium. Sweat, tears and blood mixed with the water gushing from a broken sprinkler system. Yet by 8:30, rescuers had sent to hospitals over a hundred victims, all of whom would live.

For all the lives saved by the rescue effort, it was fate more than anything else that seemed to pick and choose among the victims that night. One young woman suffered only a broken arm; her sister, standing just a few inches away, was paralyzed from the neck down. A 23-year-old hotel employee was unscathed, though the skybridges landed only seven feet from him. He describes the scene: "Glass had shredded half the body of a still-conscious young woman nearby. A man was pinned at the waist, his lower body completely flattened under one of the slabs. Some people walked into it, some walked out of it. It was unbelievable how, in that one terrible instant, so many lives were changed, or ended."

Ed Bailey, a 43-year-old lawyer, and his date, Shelley McQueeny, were pinned under both layers for several hours. Bailey heard the collapse coming, but had no time to run. "All of a sudden there was a great noise; then it was pitch-dark and we were unable to move," he remembers. "You could hear people praying, begging for help, calling for loved ones. I could feel people lying around us on both sides. They were dead. We were both in excruciating pain."

Don and Connie Downing, and their 11-year-old son, Dalton, didn't hear a thing. "One instant we were watching the dance contest and the next we were buried alive," says Connie. "It felt like a dump truck had unloaded on us." She located Dalton next to her and felt him squeeze her hand. She had no way of knowing that her husband, who had been about 10 steps ahead of them, also had survived.

Most of the victims caught directly under the bridges never had a chance. The dead ranged in age from an 11-year-old girl to an 80-year-old widower. Eighteen married couples met their doom together.

Just One More. For weeks before the disaster, Father James Flanagan, a 57-year-old Catholic priest, had been haunted by a foreboding of death. When the call came that he was needed to administer last rites at the Hyatt, he realized what his premonition had foretold. Still, when he walked into the lobby, the enormity of the scene overwhelmed him. He begged, "Please, dear God, give me strength."

Throughout that long, grim night, Father Flanagan crawled among the carnage, consoling, blessing, anointing. "Wherever I looked," he says, "someone was gravely hurt, or pleading with me to come encourage someone who was. There seemed no rhyme or reason to the pattern of destruction."

Minutes after Dr. Joseph Waeckerle, the 35-year-old chairman of emergency medicine at Baptist Memorial Hospital, arrived on the scene, he heard the voice of senior paramedic Jim Taylor: "In here! We need you in the lobby!"

The two men began a ritual that they would continue throughout the night—crawling through the rubble, seeking out the living among the mangled bodies of the dead. Later, Waeckerle spoke of the ordeal:

"It was almost dark except for a few very powerful spotlights and sparks from rescue saws and cutting torches. We were surrounded by crushed and mutilated people. All around us we heard the roar of compressors and generators, the grinding of saws and the thumping of jackhammers.

"With all the smells and sights and sounds, there was the overwhelming feeling of death. It's amazing that anybody was able to function at all, yet everybody—firemen, medics, construction workers, police, volunteers—performed magnificently."

All through that terrible night, the driving force behind the efforts of hundreds of such rescuers was the prospect of finding just one more survivor. When that happened, a rousing cheer would go up among the rescuers. It welded everyone together, the miracle of finding life amid all that death.

* * *

Precision Work. The mayor issued a single radio appeal for blood, and more than 800 people converged on the Community Blood Center of Greater Kansas City. Traffic was snarled, and at 10:30 officials announced a three-hour wait—yet the donors stayed in line and still more came.

When it was clear that rescue equipment was being stretched to the limit, construction companies and supply stores opened their doors to provide rescuers with hydraulic jacks, acetylene torches, compressors and generators. "They said, 'Take what you want,'" recalls Deputy Fire Chief Arnett Williams, who directed the department's operations that night. "I don't know if all those people got their equipment back. But no one has asked for an accounting and no one has ever submitted a bill."

At about 9:30 p.m. three huge cranes, a backhoe and several heavy-duty fork trucks—dispatched by nearby construction companies—moved like giant insects into positions at the Hyatt's main entrance and south wall. Workers looped cables around revolving doors and the backhoe yanked them loose. Sometime later the fork trucks rolled into the lobby and began gingerly removing portions of the upper skybridge. Cries from beneath the bottom layer became audible. Rescuers shouted encouragement and snaked air hoses down through the debris as they zeroed in on a victim's location.

They had expected to find a few more bodies. Instead there were 31.

Then the jackhammers went to work again, carving out openings big enough for Waeckerle to squeeze into.

"It was those jackhammers that frightened me most," says Ed Bailey. "They sounded only inches over our heads and I was terrified they would suddenly plunge through and impale us." But the rescuers handled their tools with amazing precision.

"We're getting to you!" Bailey heard a man call, and then he felt a blast of fresh air. Hands reached down, but he was still wedged too tightly to be pulled free. The forklifts growled to life and the weight lifted, the awful pressure on him suddenly gone. As the slab slowly rose, Bailey saw a woman who had been pinned next to him sit straight up and thought she was another survivor—until he saw why she had moved. "The woman was dead; her face was just glued to that concrete," he shudders. "It was then I knew how lucky Shelley and I were to be alive."

* * *

Most Horrible Moment. Trapped in a girdered "pocket" underneath two fallen sections of walkway, Connie Downing and her son Dalton heard the explosion of glass as the waiting cranes near the south end of the lobby smashed their 70-foot booms through the lobby's glass exterior. Then they heard the yelling of instructions as cables were snaked around the heaviest chunks of steel and cement. Fearing they would be crushed by the shifting of the concrete slabs, Dalton screamed for help, trying desperately to let someone know they were alive in there.

Michael Trader, a fireman working nearby, heard Dalton's cries and knelt above him in the rubble. For two hours, the fireman kept up a conversation with the boy, describing what the different threatening sounds were. It was well after two in the morning when the cranes lifted the 15,000-pound slab and jackhammers drilled an opening through to the Downings. They were free. At 4:30 a.m. the last living victim was pulled from beneath what had once been part of a skybridge, bringing the total number to survive under both layers to seven. Yet workers continued through the rest of the gray morning hours, carefully lifting and setting aside one slab after another, hoping for yet another survivor.

Then, at approximately 7:30 a.m., with a light drizzle falling outside, came what most rescuers remember as the most horrible moment of all. After nine hours of mighty labor, the final section of fallen skybridge was raised and moved aside by the cranes. They had expected to find a few more bodies. Instead there were 31.

"The rescuers were visibly shaken," Father Flanagan recalls. "It seemed to drain the last ounces of their strength."

The final toll: more than 300 casualties, 114 of them deaths. Federal authorities called the disaster "in terms of loss of life and injuries ... the most devastating structural collapse ever to take place in the United States."

In Kansas City the shock was all the more stunning because it was such a concentrated tragedy. Unlike most disasters—an air crash or a hotel fire where the victims are usually from far-flung places—more than 90% of the dead were from the area. It seems everyone in Kansas City knew someone who was there, had thought of going or had been at another tea dance there. "It was," said Mayor Richard L. Berkley, "like a death in the family."

*   *   *

Fatal Flaw. At the National Bureau of Standards (NBS), the federal agency charged with studying structural performances and special failures, samples of the skybridges—obtained by court permission—were subjected to a wide range of structural tests. The experts found neither the workmanship nor the quality of materials of significance in initiating the collapse. The fatal flaws, they concluded, lay with a fault in the original design and in a structural design change made during construction.

As the second- and fourth-floor skybridges were originally planned, both were to be suspended from the ceiling by continuous 1¼-inch hanger rods. Their construction would be possible but time-consuming. Some-where along the line, someone decided to make that construction easier. The simpler design suspended the upper skybridge from the ceiling as planned. But the lower tier was suspended from the fourth-floor tier—essentially doubling the load at crucial points on both the upper and lower walkways. From the day it was built, the NBS report makes clear, the sky-bridge structure was barely able to support its own weight, not to mention that of the people watching the dance contest. It was a structure that was doomed to fall, and it did so at the worst possible moment.

Who is to blame? Drawings showing the plan change for supporting the skybridges were prepared by the hotel's steel fabricator and reviewed by the architect, the structural engineer and the general contractor. Yet, according to Edward O. Pfrang, who headed the NBS study, "almost any practicing engineer could easily have seen that the skybridges would not meet the Kansas City building code."

The design change was not, in fact, either reported or reviewed by city building inspectors since this was not required by the city code. Yet even the original skybridge design that *was* approved by city building inspectors did not satisfy the design requirements of the city's building code, according to the NBS study, and a private study commissioned by the city government after the Hyatt disaster urged a reexamination of the role of all parties in shared responsibility for the safety of major projects.

Meanwhile, more than $3 billion in lawsuits had been filed.

Could this tragedy be repeated? Many authorities warn that the factors which contributed to the Kansas City disaster could well exist elsewhere, and local officials have been urged to systematically reexamine building-code procedures.

Just two months before the Hyatt collapse, the American Institute of Architects (AIA) had completed a study of "long-span" structures which appeared to be particularly vulnerable to disaster—a study spurred in part by the collapse in recent years of the $30-million Civic Center Coliseum in Hartford, Connecticut; the $12.2-million Kemper Memorial Arena in Kansas City; and the Rosemont Horizon Arena, a $19-million sports complex near Chicago. The loss of life in these accidents was low because the structures were empty of spectators. But the report warned that "if there is a next time, we may not be so lucky." Although directed at long-span designs, AIA's prescient warning applies to any structure that lacks backup supports, as did the Kansas City Hyatt.

On Oct. 1, 1981, the hotel reopened after a three-month, $5-million renovation program. A blue-ribbon technical committee had gone through every inch of the building, making design-change recommendations. Roofs and walls were strengthened, and fireproofing was upgraded. In place of the skybridges is a single, sturdy balcony supported by 10 massive, reinforced-concrete columns that are anchored on bedrock. The Kansas City Hyatt is probably one of the safest buildings in the world today. It is hard to believe that tragedy occurred there.

But memory of that gruesome night remains very much on people's minds in Kansas City. "It's a night no one will ever forget," says McMullin. "It's one that cannot be allowed to repeat itself, anywhere, ever again."

Originally published in July 1982 issue of *Reader's Digest* magazine.

Special thanks to Robert Macy, an Associated Press correspondent, who was at the scene and who helped with the preparation of this article.

Humor Hall of Fame

I feel so lucky to be a writer's assistant but so unlucky that a room full of people have to watch me try to type the word lieutenant.

—@LIBBYDOYNE

I was interviewing a young woman who had applied for a job in our gift shop. It turned out that her favorite sport was soccer, and she was bending my ear about her accomplishments in the neighborhood league. Trying to steer the interview back to her job qualifications, I asked, "So, tell me about your long-range goals." After thinking a minute, she replied, "Once I kicked the ball in from midfield."

—RALPH J. STEINITZ

Working for a florist, I took a call from a woman who spoke to me over a very crackly cell phone. She wanted to send a wreath to a friend's funeral, but I couldn't make out what message she wanted to accompany the flowers. Finally, I just had to interrupt her. "It's a bad line," I said over the din. There was a slight pause before she said, "Well, can you think of something better to say?"

—IVOR EDWARDS

"It's for the boss. He's having a really bad day."

She Rode to Triumph Over Polio

by Edwin Muller

With relentless determination, one might be surprised at what is possible

At the horse show in New York there was one exhibition that always brought down the house. The lights in Madison Square Garden would go out. Two spotlights would focus on a single rider, a pretty, dark-haired woman in her mid-30's who rode her horse as if she were part of it, performing a sequence of intricate, delicate steps and movements: turning, backing, changing from trot to canter to gallop.

It was a performance of what the horse fraternity calls "dressage," and it requires more riding ability than the jumps or any other part of the horseman's art. The horse is guided by imperceptible, perfectly coordinated movements of the rider's legs, hands, body—by balance and a subtle shift of weight.

Those in the audience who applauded most were the connoisseurs. They realized what a remarkable feat of horsemanship they had seen. But only a few of them understood what a truly extraordinary achievement it had been. Behind it lies a shining story of courage and unconquerable human will.

Lis Hartel at the Equestrian Games in Stockholm with horse Jubilee

The rider was Madame Lis Hartel of Copenhagen. Ten years before she had been struck down by polio. It was a bad case, the sort from which, if the patient recovers, he is lucky to be only partially crippled for life.

Her doctor tried to encourage her. He said that if she strove hard she might eventually be able to walk with two canes.

Lis meant to do more. She meant to ride again. At that the doctor could only smile.

In September 1944, Lis Hartel was young, healthy and strong. Happily married, she had a baby of two, another on the way. She was one of the best riders in Denmark. It was good to be alive.

Then came the sickening wave of realization: those muscles were now dead.

One Monday morning she woke with a terrific headache and a curious stiffness in the back of her neck. A few days later the paralysis began—clutching her arms and legs, creeping over her body. They took her to the hospital. It was hard to fight down panic, to keep a grip on herself, not to go to pieces and scream. Being pregnant made it worse. She was in terror for the baby, even though doctors and nurses told her that it would probably be born normal, which often happened with polio patients. As for herself—well, of course she would never be normal again. They talked brightly of the future day when she would be up on crutches.

Still, here in the hospital she would dream sometimes that she was riding again as she had from childhood, guiding the horse by the familiar movements of thighs and knee muscles. Then came the sickening wave of realization: those muscles were now dead.

Most people would have resigned themselves to that. But Lis Hartel has a fighting heart. Her body lay there—helpless, beaten down. But her spirit wasn't beaten. Resolve grew strong within her.

In the third week she demanded that she leave the hospital. The campaign that she planned could be fought better at home.

At home she had two strong allies: her husband and her mother. Lis Hartel insists that without them she would have been beaten.

Together they planned a regime. There was the usual therapy: massage, electric treatment. But far more important were the things that she had to do for herself.

Over her bed they rigged a system of cords and pulleys. Cords were attached to her hand and feet; they ran over pulleys on the ceiling and had balancing weights on the other end. The tiniest movement of a muscle would have lifted an arm or leg. But for many days the strongest effort of her will couldn't induce that tiny movement.

Then one day came a glimmer of hope. She had been trying and trying to lift her right arm. Suddenly it moved. She wept with joy. There was a family celebration.

But next day the arm wouldn't move. That is the way things went for weeks—small movements of arms or legs, then a relapse to inertness. She drove herself at it, day after day; but progress was infinitely slow.

When she was able, fairly consistently, to make slight movements of arms or legs, and when she could sit up, they tried something else. Two gymnasium bicycling machines were fixed to the floor, arranged so that the pedaling of one made the pedals of the other go round. Lis sat on one, her husband or her mother on the other.

It was exhausting work—and she was pregnant. After a few minutes of it she would have to be put back in bed. But as the weeks went on, the thigh muscles gradually came under some control.

These daily exercises went on for months, hour after hour. Then an interruption—the birth of her baby. It was an anxious time for the family but, as the doctor had predicted, all went well. The new daughter was normal and healthy. And after a while Lis could go back to her regime.

She was almost in collapse when she was put back to bed. But she managed to crawl a few inches.

Then there was crawling. She was laid face down on the floor. A towel was put under her body, husband and mother each holding an end. They lifted her slightly from the floor and she strove to crawl forward.

This was the most exhausting of all. She was almost in collapse when she was put back to bed. But she managed to crawl a few inches. As she improved she set herself the goal of crawling a yard further each day.

Next came the efforts to walk—long continued before she was able to take a single step. At last she could manage a few painful steps on crutches. Then, eight months after the attack, she could hobble along with two crutch canes.

Her friends congratulated her. It was what they had hoped for. Obviously they thought that her battle was now concluded, that she had reached the furthest point of recovery which she could possibly expect.

Lis Hartel thought otherwise.

In a war there are two kinds of generals. One, after winning a battle, pauses to consolidate his position, is content for the moment with the ground he has won. The other doesn't pause for an instant, presses on relentlessly, is satisfied with nothing less than the complete rout of the enemy. Lis Hartel is the second kind.

Now she broached a project that she had long had in mind. Her family members were doubtful about it, but they finally agreed.

One morning she was taken in her wheelchair to the stables. Her horse Gigolo was saddled. She was lifted up.

She rode constantly, steadily improving her form. She was a better rider than she had been before her illness.

She knew what would happen. When the horse started to walk her instinctive fear of falling off would stir to life long-dead reflexes in the muscles of her thighs. Feebly her legs gripped the horse. It wasn't enough. She toppled, but she tried it again. And again.

After it she was nearer collapse than ever before. She rested two weeks, then tried again. Once she was close to giving up. She had them pack away her riding kit.

"I'm through," she said.

But next day she had the kit unpacked again.

At last came the day when she could keep her seat on Gigolo without help. The thigh muscles grew stronger. Her balance improved. One day she could keep her seat at a trot.

In 1946, two years after her attack, she watched the Scandinavian riding championships. In the paddock were many old friends from her days of competition.

She told them:

"Next year I'll be riding with you."

They pretended to believe her.

But she *was* there next year—riding in competition, three years after the polio had struck. She still had to be helped on and off the horse but, once up, she rode like a champion. To the amazement of those who knew about her condition, she won second prize in the women's dressage event.

That did not content her. She would be satisfied with nothing less than total victory. She went on with her regime of exercises, strenuous and unremitting.

By now she had a normal body once more, except that below the knees the muscles were paralyzed. She studied and practiced how to do without those muscles. Now, after two operations, she walked with just one cane.

She rode constantly, steadily improving her form. She was a better rider than she had been before her illness. Indeed, she had become one of the best riders in the world.

That was proved at the Olympic Games of 1952, held in Helsinki. There, in the dressage event, Lis Hartel competed with the 24 top-ranking riders from all over the world, men and women. She won second prize, the silver medal.

When she stood up to have the prize awarded, when the Danish flag was run up over the stadium, when the crowd roared its applause, she broke down and wept.

Since then she has ridden in competition and performed in many countries, making four or five appearances a year. She does it not merely because she enjoys riding more than any other activity. There is another reason.

She wants to help other polio victims. If they see the evidence of how she has made herself get well, they may be inspired to do the same for themselves.

Lis Hartel answers hundreds of letters from polio victims each year. What she says and writes is:

"Never give up. However dark it may look, there is almost always a chance of making some progress which may be a milestone toward recovery. Keep on trying to do better. You can do almost anything if you only believe it hard enough."

Originally published in August 1955 issue of *Reader's Digest* magazine.

If you always worry
about what's ahead, you
always pass up today.
So you know what
I stick to? I stick to joy.
Just joy.

—RUSSELL WILSON
Football player in the *New York Times*

"I've Found Gold!"

by Fergus M. Bordewich

When the word got out, a multitude
of fortune seekers raced to California—
and America was changed forever

While inspecting the watercourse of a sawmill in Northern California, carpenter James Marshall caught sight of a glittering object. Something metallic was shining a few inches under the rippling surface of the American River's South Fork. Marshall soon realized he'd stumbled on something very rare. "By God," he said of his discovery that January day in 1848, "I believe I have found a gold mine!"

Marshall went to find his employer, a Swiss adventurer named John Sutter, whose 48,000-acre land grant encompassed some of the best farmland in California. Marshall locked the door, opened a scrap of cotton cloth and placed the gold on the table.

The men tried to keep the discovery secret, Sutter staying at his fort while Marshall raced back to the sawmill. After a restless night, Sutter met him upriver, where Sutter used his pocketknife to pry loose a nugget that weighed an ounce and a half. Before sundown, the two had filled their pockets.

GOLD ON THE BRAIN

At the port of Yerba Buena (soon renamed San Francisco), the news caused a sensation. Sam Brannan, an enterprising merchant who had a general store at Sutter's fort, walked along Montgomery Street holding up vials of gold dust, shouting, "Gold! Gold! From the American River!" Doctors, judges, clerks and soldiers raced for the gold fields. Stores shut, newspapers closed and ships were deserted by their crews. "The fever set in and gold was on the brain," said one miner.

The gold seekers poured onto Sutter's land. When Brannan's general store ran out of supplies, they began stealing tools, food, livestock and gold itself. Sutter, once hopeful he would become the richest man in California, now struggled to maintain his land.

The rush is on! From April 1849 to the end of that year, 31,000 arrived by ship in San Francisco. "Farewell my parents, farewell my brothers all," many sang, in the words of a popular tune. "I'm going to California, I'm answering the call."

Prospectors quickly discovered that gold deposits stretched for 120 miles—from the Feather River in the north almost to the Tuolumne River in the south, and 60 miles from west to east. The first miners didn't even bother to stake claims—they just scooped up the surface gold, then moved on. Stories abounded. On the Yuba River, one man picked up 30 pounds of gold from a four-foot-square area. Another found $2,000 worth of gold under his doorstep.

When President James K. Polk confirmed the discovery in December 1848, the gold rush began in earnest. Tens of thousands of Americans and foreigners prepared to head to California. "The gold rush energized the nation," wrote J.S. Holliday, author of *The World Rushed In*. "It seemed to confirm the American dream of limitless opportunity."

RISKY BUSINESS

Between April and December 1849, 31,000 people arrived by ship in San Francisco. But most forty-niners chose the overland route—a four-to-six-month journey across 2,000 miles of largely unmapped wilderness. One of them was Englishman James Hutchings, 24, a journalist working in New Orleans. As he journeyed westward, he kept a detailed diary.

May 16, 1849: "*Ho for California!" was the general cry, and it suited my taste to go.*

Hutchings went by steamboat to St. Joseph, Missouri, where he joined a company of men who pooled their money to purchase wagons, oxen,

Fortune seekers. Forty-niners such as these dug, scraped and sifted, searching for the gleaming grains that would change their lives. Workers accustomed to average salaries of $60 a month had been dazzled by accurate reports that a man with ordinary luck could make $500 a month.

tools and food for the trek to California. Crossing the prairie, Hutchings saw long trains of wagons, their white canvas covers stretching away for miles. Soon he began passing the graves of those who had died along the way, most of them from cholera.

June 23: Without water for 25 miles. I became so thirsty as to be sick and giddy. I came to a deep wheel rut with water no warmer than new milk, drank deeply, rested and drank again.

Flat prairie gave way to the rugged landscape of the West, and Hutchings's company traveled by starlight to avoid the daytime heat. At first the Native Americans they encountered were not hostile. But as the newcomers began killing off game and intruding in ever-greater numbers, the Native Americans started stealing the immigrants' livestock. Bloody encounters increased.

September 23: About midnight I heard a whickering among the horses, and saw the head of an Indian. With my revolver cocked, I started after him to get a favorable shot, but couldn't do it. We went looking for the animals, and to our great dismay six of them were missing.

October 3: A team just ahead of us picked up a white man, dead, with five arrows in his side.

The forbidding peaks of the Sierras now rose up before the exhausted men. In mid-October, weak and hungry, Hutchings descended to a chaotic sprawl of tents and log cabins that was his dream: the mining camp of Hangtown. It was so named because of the swift way its inhabitants dealt with troublemakers.

...ng the amount ...
...ife" which is required for an eigh
trip in the mountains:

8 lbs potatoes.
1 bottle whisky.
1 bottle pepper sauce.
1 bottle whisky.
1 box tea.
9 lbs onions.
2 bottles whisky.
1 ham.
11 lbs crackers.
1 bottle whisky.
½ doz. sardines.
2 bottles brandy, (4th proof.)
6 lbs sugar.
1 bottle brandy, (4th proof.)
7 lbs cheese.
2 bottles brandy, (4th proof.)
1 bottle pepper.
5 gallons whisky.
4 bottles whisky (old Bourbon.)
1 small keg whisky.
1 bottle of cocktails, (designed "starter.")

Shopping list. *The necessities required for eight days in the mining camps, as published in 1860*

"With a washbowl on my knee..."
A typical miner with his washbowl,
in a rare daguerreotype

LAWLESS WORLD

By then, almost 100,000 forty-niners were crowding into the gold fields. Hutchings described his first attempts: *Properly equipped with pickax, shovel and pan, I tried my fortune and made $5.70. It doesn't do to become discouraged but work on in hope.*

The miners dug, scraped and sifted for the gleaming grains that would change their lives. In the process, they threw up helter-skelter towns with such names as Hog Eye, You Bet and Pinch 'em Tight. The air rang with the shouts and curses of men in a dozen European and Indian languages. The gold rush created a rough world, without government or clergy—and with few women.

Louise Clappe, a petite young woman from New Jersey, followed her doctor husband to the hell-raising camp of Rich Bar. In a letter to her sister back East, she wrote: *The news spreads that wonderful "diggings" have been discovered at such a place. Those worse than fiends rush vulture-like upon the scene and erect a round tent, wherein gambling, drinking, swearing and fighting, the many reproduce Pandemonium in more than its original horror.*

In the early months crime was almost nonexistent, since it was as easy to find gold as steal it. Heaps were left unguarded inside tents or thrown on hillsides while men worked. But as gold grew harder to find, violence became epidemic. *In 24 days,* Clappe wrote, *we have had murders, fearful accidents, bloody deaths, a mob, whippings, a hanging—and a fatal duel.*

Changing America forever. The gold rush ultimately transformed a remote strip of coastline into the most populous state in our nation. It inspired the first cross-country mail routes, the pony express, the transcontinental telegraph and, eventually, the transcontinental railroad. Between 1848 and 1880, California gold poured $2 billion ($60 billion today) into America's economy.

In the lawless atmosphere, miners killed Native Americans and seized their lands. Slave hunters raided their villages, taking women and children. The Native American population before the gold rush was probably more than 150,000; in 1870 it was 30,000.

WINNERS AND LOSERS

The greatest fortunes were made not by those with pans but those with ledgers. In a land where a boiled egg sold for 75 cents, flour for $2 a pound and boots for $35, a canny businessman could amass wealth with astonishing speed.

One merchant who did work the mines was Leland Stanford from

Watervliet, New York. When he secured possession of a gold mine, Stanford and the foreman took a pan and pickax, entered the tunnel and started chopping. The ecstatic Stanford found 76 ounces of gold. Eventually, $50,000 worth of gold was extracted from a space less than 12 feet square.

The mine proved to be one of California's richest. Earnings from it provided Stanford a steppingstone to the governorship of California and to the U.S. Senate. Later, when his son died at age 15, Stanford honored him by converting his Palo Alto horse farm into a college. Chelsea Clinton, daughter of the former President Bill Clinton, attended Stanford University.

But what became of those less celebrated California dreamers? Louise Clappe moved to San Francisco and became a beloved schoolteacher; she eventually retired to New Jersey, her birthplace.

After digging two months, James Hutchings amassed several thousand dollars' worth of gold and deposited it in a bank. But the bank collapsed and Hutchings lost everything. Undaunted, he moved on and again struck gold—$8,000 worth (equal to $136,000 today). He invested this money in his own publishing enterprise and earned a second fortune as a chronicler of life in the mining camps. He remained in Yosemite, California, throughout his career.

While John Sutter seemed destined for wealth and glory, his gold came to nothing. Miners overran his property and tore

Gold beyond the hills. In the 1850s, a canny businessman could make a bundle. This merchant, named Levi Strauss, built his own private gold mine by selling dry goods wholesale at his San Francisco store. He later went on to patent denim work trousers that became known as Levi's.

apart his mill for equipment. By the end of 1849, virtually everything Sutter owned had been stolen. Not until 1864 did the California state legislature vote him a stipend of $3,000 per year.

James Marshall, who found the first nugget, wandered the gold fields for years, followed by newcomers convinced he had a magical ability to find gold. But he never did again. When he died in 1885, his property was auctioned off to pay his debts. It brought $150.

Today the green water of the American River's South Fork still rushes over the rocks where a gleam of gold had caught James Marshall's eye. And if you close your eyes and listen, you can still hear the dim clink of picks, the scrape of gravel and the shouts of discovery: "Gold! Gold! I've found it!"

Originally published in February 1998 issue of *Reader's Digest* magazine.

If my dogs are happy, I'm happy. That sounds like something my mother used to say about her children, which I thought was … way overstated. I was wrong.

—ISAAC MIZRAHI
Designer in *Vanity Fair*

Humor Hall of Fame

Time is a great healer. That's why they make you wait so long in the doctor's office.

—RON DENTINGER

My dentist's office was in the midst of renovation when I arrived for a checkup. As the hygienist led me to a room, I could hear the sound of hammering and sawing coming from next door. "It must really scare your patients to hear that when they're in the dentist's chair," I remarked.

"That's nothing," she said. "You should see what happens when they hear the jackhammer."

—CHUCK ROTHMAN

Hospital regulations require a wheelchair for patients being discharged. However, while working as a student nurse, I found one elderly gentleman already dressed and sitting on the bed with a suitcase at his feet—who insisted he didn't need my help to leave the hospital. After a chat about rules being rules, he reluctantly let me wheel him to the elevator. On the way down I asked if his wife was meeting him. "I don't know," he said. "She's still upstairs in the bathroom changing out of her hospital gown."

—PATSY R. DANCEY

"What do you mean I have an ulcer? I give ulcers, I don't get them!"

STEPPING UP TO THE PLATE

I coached my son's Little League team. We lost every game until
the last. In the final inning, we were in the field, ahead by 1 with
no outs and the bases loaded. The batter hit a line drive right to
our third baseman. She stuck out her glove with one hand and
covered her eyes with the other. The ball landed in her glove.
She jumped up and down, stomping on third base to make the
second out. Then she stuck out her glove to show me the ball,
tagging the runner coming in—an unassisted triple play! Our
team ran to the pitcher's mound in celebration as if it were the
World Series.

—Robert Drozel, *Exton, PA*

WHEN THE GOING GETS TOUGH ...

My daughter was very competitive growing up, but she was
smaller than most kids, so I was always protective. Once, during
an intense basketball game against an aggressive team, she got
hit in the face pretty hard with the ball. From the second row,
I jumped up to help her. She saw, pointed and yelled "No,
Mom!" and played on. That was the day I learned she'd be
just fine.

—Kristine Berglund, *Aledo, IL*

The Key Witness

by Lynn Rosellini

Being a good citizen and telling the truth makes one man an everyday hero

The cabdriver was living the American dream. He had fled the violence in his native Sudan in 1999 and had come to the United States, settling in North Carolina because he'd heard it was warm, like Africa. He sent money home to his parents every month, first from his job delivering pizza and then from wages at an IBM factory. But Moezeldin Elmostafa had bigger dreams—of opening his own business and bringing his wife and three children to live with him. In 2004 he started a taxi service with a friend. He could not have imagined that, two years later, a late night fare would put him at the center of a notorious legal case.

Durham, North Carolina, is a college town, and Elmostafa, 38, was a familiar sight as he shuttled students between Duke University and other campuses in his bright red On Time Taxi van. Passengers liked the friendly, soft-spoken driver, and his Sudanese buddies admired his honesty and work ethic. It wasn't unusual, shortly after midnight on March 14, 2006, when a call came in from a student requesting Elmostafa's cab.

When Elmostafa arrived at the corner of Watts and Urban Avenues, two young men, dressed in T-shirts and shorts and clearly in a post-party mood, piled in. Joking and laughing, they directed Elmostafa to an ATM, then to a drive-through restaurant. Finally, Elmostafa delivered them

Cabdriver Moezeldin Elmostafa risked all for the truth.

to Duke's West Campus. The fare was $17, but they gave him $25. Nice tip, he thought. He picked up one more passenger that night, then went home to bed.

A month later, the phone rang at On Time Taxi. It was an attorney representing Reade Seligmann, one of three Duke University lacrosse players charged with sexually assaulting an exotic dancer during an off-campus party. At the time of the alleged crime, Seligmann said, he was riding in Elmostafa's cab.

Although the Duke rape case had captured the nation's attention, Elmostafa didn't follow the news, preferring to spend his free time barbecuing on his deck. But he knew one thing: He didn't want to get involved in a criminal trial. He loved his new country, from McDonald's hamburgers to Court TV. Most of all, he loved the opportunity here.

"You can start from nothing in America," he had told friends, "and you can be something." He had applied for citizenship and worried that being a witness in court might jeopardize his chances.

When the lacrosse player showed up with his father a few days later, Elmostafa immediately recognized the burly, 6-foot-1-inch student. "My son didn't do anything," Philip Seligmann said. "His whole life is in front of him." Could Elmostafa vouch for the ride?

The taxi driver thought of his own 2-year-old son, Mohammed, back in Sudan. He hoped the boy would grow up in America, maybe become a doctor. How could he let this other man's son go to jail?

"I will testify," he said. "I will stand up and tell the whole truth." Elmostafa swore out an affidavit and even produced a cell phone bill that listed a call from Reade Seligmann's phone at 12:14 a.m. on the day of the alleged assault. The cabbie repeated his story to detectives.

Two weeks later, the same detectives showed up at the taxi office with a warrant for his arrest. Elmostafa was confused. Hadn't he done everything you're supposed to do in America? Hadn't he told the truth? Kamal Balal, his business partner, watched police take his friend away in handcuffs.

Elmostafa's heart pounded during the ride downtown. In Sudan people could be arrested for next to nothing and sometimes languished in jail for years without a trial.

At the station, Elmostafa was booked on a misdemeanor larceny charge. It dated back to September 2003, when he'd driven a woman to a department store, waited for her in his taxi and then driven her home. The woman later pleaded guilty to shoplifting $250 in handbags from the store. Elmostafa told investigators he was unaware of what his passenger had done.

The case had been settled more than two years earlier, Elmostafa thought. *Why were police dragging it out again now?* As he sat in jail, waiting for Balal to arrive with the $750 bail, he began to fit the pieces together. By the time he walked out, five hours later, he was steaming.

"They're trying to scare me so I'll change my testimony in the Duke case!" he told Balal. Police claimed his arrest was not unusual, saying they routinely investigate witnesses who may be called to trial.

Durham County District Attorney Michael Nifong was already under fire for using strong-arm tactics. Elmostafa was determined not to be intimidated. He hired a lawyer, bought a new white dress shirt and faced the misdemeanor charges in August 2006. He was acquitted.

Eight months later, the Duke lacrosse players were cleared of all charges too. Jim Cooney, Seligmann's attorney, called Elmostafa "one of the great heroes of this case." Cooney lauded the taxi driver for refusing to be cowed. "He told the truth under oath, exactly the way we expect a citizen of this country to do."

DA Nifong was disbarred after a North Carolina State Bar disciplinary panel found him guilty of ethics violations, including withholding key DNA evidence from the young men's attorneys.

As for Elmostafa, he owes a friend $2,500 for attorney fees. But the experience hasn't soured him on America. If anything, he says, it demonstrated a criminal justice system that works. He's passed his citizenship exam and is waiting to be called to take the oath. "I'm looking forward to being a good citizen."

Originally published in November 2007 issue of *Reader's Digest* magazine.

Tidying up means
dealing with all the
"things" in your life.
So what do you really
want to put in order?

—MARIE KONDO,
Tidying expert in the book
Marie Kondo's Kurashi at Home

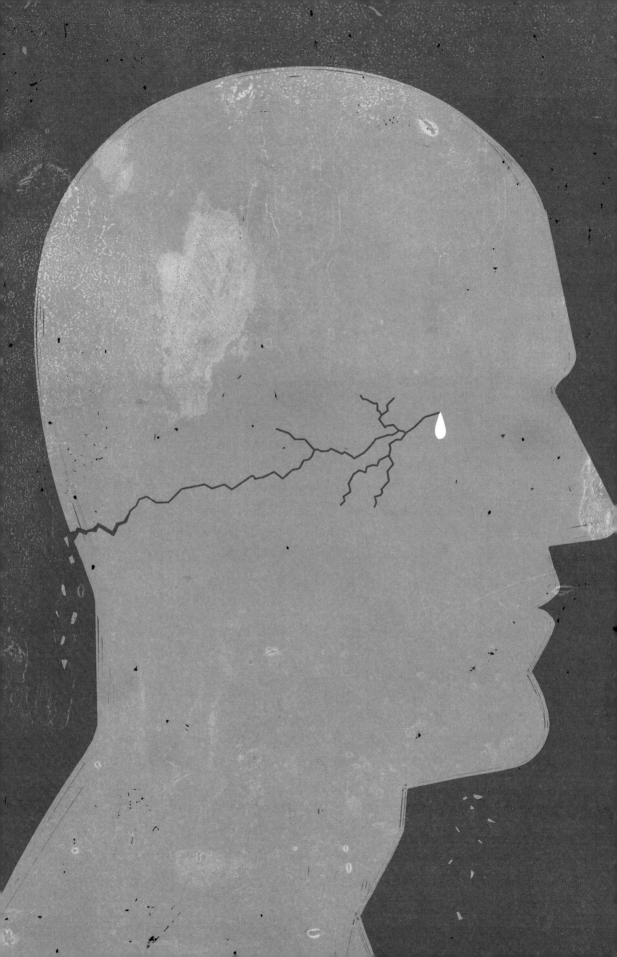

The 39-Year-Old Apology

by Tom Hallman Jr., from the *Oregonian*

A bond was broken by a thoughtless act years ago. Could all be forgiven with a simple "I'm sorry"?

W hen he was 12 years old, the boy did something he only later realized probably hurt his seventh-grade teacher. It was minor—he was, after all, a kid. But in time, when he was older and wiser, he wanted to find this teacher and apologize. But the teacher seemed to have vanished. Over the decades, the boy—Larry Israelson, now a man—occasionally turned to the internet, typing the teacher's name into search boxes. He never found anything. But he never quit looking. Nearly 39 years after the event happened, he got a hit.

Stunned, he started reading a story I had written in the *Oregonian* about a program that helps at-risk kids. He studied an accompanying photograph and recognized his teacher, who was a volunteer. He then emailed me:

You published an item involving retired teacher James Atteberry. Mr. Atteberry was a teacher of mine in the early '70s, and I wish to apologize to him for a regrettable incident that occurred when I was his student. Would you be willing to serve as an intermediary and deliver a message on my behalf?

I contacted Atteberry. Intrigued, he told me to respond to this former student and see what happened. Shortly thereafter, I received an overnight package containing a sealed envelope, which I then forwarded to Atteberry.

When I mentioned this letter to people, they all reacted in the same way: They each had someone they wished they could apologize to. And they told me that by the time they realized that truth, it was too late.

In my case, it was someone who has haunted me for decades.

My third-grade teacher had organized a Christmas gift exchange. On the big day, we sat in a circle, taking turns ripping open a fancy package containing a new toy. Then it was my turn. The teacher handed me something that had been wrapped in paper that was clearly reused. It was so wrinkled and retaped that the colors had faded. With everyone watching, I peeled back the paper and pulled out a cheap paperback book with torn and dirty pages.

Tucked inside was a handwritten note identifying the girl who gave it to me. When I announced her name, my classmates started laughing. Her gift was yet another indication of just how different this girl was from the rest of us. She'd arrive late to class, her hair wet and unkempt.

When it comes to saying sorry, no one gets a pass. Everyone deserves an apology.

She didn't have friends, and the popular students made fun of her because she was poor and wore old clothes.

Even though this incident happened nearly 50 years ago, I remember that afternoon as if it were yesterday. As the class laughed, this 8-year-old girl turned in her chair to hide her tears while the teacher unsuccessfully tried to restore order in a class that had turned on the weakest among us.

At that moment, I was worried that the popular kids would think that this girl and I were friends. So I didn't thank her or even acknowledge the

Teacher and student: James Atteberry and Larry Israelson, around 1973.

gift. Only decades later—like Larry Israelson—did I realize that what I did next was unforgivable: I tossed the book in the garbage.

For years I wanted to apologize. So while waiting to see what became of Israelson and Atteberry, I typed her name into an internet search field. I found nothing. I realized then why Israelson was so intent on finding Atteberry. It was all about getting a second chance.

*   *   *

As James Atteberry read the letter, he was brought back to 1973, when he was a middle school history and composition teacher in Huntington Beach, just south of Los Angeles. He was 37, got great reviews and was well liked. He was also gay.

"If a teacher was found to be gay, his contract would not be renewed," Atteberry said. "Gay teachers kept their mouths shut. People of this era might not understand it. But it was an intense time. An art teacher in

CLASS REUNION. *Reader's Digest* arranged for James Atteberry (right) and Larry Israelson to meet after 40 years. The former teacher arrived early at the hotel lounge. He sat peering at everyone to see if he could recognize his old student. Then he spotted a tall man ambling toward him. "What happened to that little guy?" he asked, smiling.

"He grew up," said Larry Israelson.

After a long hug and some catching up, Atteberry jumped into the subject that had brought them together in July—that article published in *The Oregonian*. "I was puzzled why you left the class. I knew it wasn't because you were rotten," Atteberry said with a laugh. "It was survival. In junior high, it is survival of the fittest."

Both men voiced surprise over the attention the article had received—the calls, letters and emails sent their way from around the world.

"The takeaway is optimism," reasoned Israelson. "There are universal themes of an apology sought and forgiveness granted."

At the end of their reunion—which included lunch with Israelson's wife, Conny—Israelson accepted an invitation to visit Atteberry and his partner.

"How wonderful it is that we can go back into our past," said Atteberry later. "All of this has made me think about what a wonderful life I have lived."

the school made a stupid mistake, and that was the end of his career. I never talked about my life."

And yes, he told me, he remembered Larry Israelson.

I am truly sorry for asking to be transferred out of your seventh-grade social studies class during the 1972–73 school year. I don't have many memories from school, but at the top of one of my assignments you wrote "You will go far in life. Your command of the English language is exceptional." Looking back on my younger self, I am certain that I reveled in being one of the teacher's pets. As comfortable as I was in a classroom, however, the boy's locker room was something else entirely.

On the phone, Larry Israelson's voice is low, strong and confident. He stands, he says, 6 feet 5 inches and played water polo in high school and in college.

"But when I was 12," he said, "I was a scrawny little kid who was into books. A lot of the athletic guys loved to tease those of us who were weak. You know what it is to feel powerless?"

Some students suspected Atteberry was gay. A boy in class asked Atteberry what he thought about a proposed law banning gay teachers. When Atteberry asked the boy why he'd posed the question, the student said his father had specifically told him to ask Atteberry. The teacher chose his words carefully.

Israelson was one of his best students. Bright and articulate, he submitted essays that Atteberry thought were remarkably good. "I would praise Larry in class," Atteberry said. "That was his downfall."

In the locker room, boys began picking on Israelson.

"They started saying 'Larry' and then 'fairy' and rhyming it with 'Atteberry,'" Israelson recalled.

When he pleaded with them to stop, he was challenged to a fight.

"I took a couple of hard punches," he said. "I gave up."

The teasing intensified, with the taunts becoming more sexually explicit and graphic. Israelson told no one. One day, when he could no longer stand it, he showed up at the principal's office and said he needed to leave Atteberry's class. The principal couldn't understand why, but he eventually signed a transfer slip and handed it to Israelson. The student walked into Atteberry's classroom, interrupted the lesson, and handed Atteberry the slip. Without a word, Israelson gathered his books and walked out the door.

"There was no goodbye, no explanation," Israelson said. "I just disappeared. I never talked to Mr. Atteberry again."

*　*　*

When it comes to apologies, no one gets a pass in this life. Everyone deserves one, and everyone needs to give one.

When Israelson married, he was the first Anglo to marry into a Mexican-American family. More than a decade into the marriage—by this time, he and his wife, Conny, had two daughters—his brother-in-law invited him out for a beer. After some small talk, his brother-in-law took a deep breath and got to the point.

"He apologized," Israelson said. "He said that he hadn't wanted an Anglo in the family. He'd lobbied behind the scenes to try to get his sister to break up with me. He said he'd felt bad about it for all these years and decided it was time to make it right."

That phrase made Israelson think of Atteberry. The man had inspired and encouraged Israelson at a time when a compliment or praise scrawled across the top of an essay so mattered in a boy's young life. He thought about what it must have been like for Atteberry to hide who he was. Israelson intensified his search. A decade later, he found my story.

*　*　*

Israelson had been writing an imaginary letter to Atteberry for over 30 years. But now he struggled to find the right words. He was "truly sorry" for asking to be transferred, he wrote. "I know my age was a mitigating factor, but when I replayed this incident in my adult head, it shamed me."

He sealed the envelope and sent it to me to be forwarded to Atteberry.

He expected nothing more. He had done what he had set out to do, and now it was over.

When Atteberry read the letter, he, too, remembered what it had been like to be a boy. Like Israelson, he had been bullied. Two athletes had grabbed him when he was walking home, forced him to pull down his pants and whipped him with a belt. Shamed, he told no one, the matter made worse when the athletes tormented him by demanding each day that he turn over his lunch money to them.

In a strange way, this letter allowed Atteberry to come to terms with his own past. He was not alone.

Atteberry had always wondered why Israelson had left his class. Was it something he did or said to this student? Now he knew.

He set the letter aside, went to his computer, and typed Israelson's name into a search box. He found the address and a telephone number.

One thousand miles away, a phone rang. A man answered.

"Larry," a voice on the other end said, "this is your teacher."

Originally published in October 2012 issue of *Reader's Digest* magazine.

Lush Environment

Welcome to one of the wettest places on Earth. It rains more than an inch a day here, which gives the area its green coat. But that cloak also hides a historic scar: A bloody battle back in 1790 ended with warriors attempting to make a stand atop the leftmost peak, among the most sacred destinations in the state. Where is it?

A. Paradise, Michigan

B. Iao Valley State Monument, Hawaii

C. Snoqualmie Falls, Washington

D. Tongass National Forest, Alaska

Answer on page 287. *Photograph by shutterjack/Getty Images*

Terror at the Beach

by Lisa Fitterman | Derek Burnett

Chilling real-life dramas at a popular spot for fun

1. SHARK ATTACK!

The clear blue water of the Pacific Ocean looks so inviting. Sitting by the campfire, Denis Udovenko strums his guitar impatiently. He wants to go for an early-evening swim, but his wife, Polina, is fussing with pots and pans at their beach campsite in tiny Telyakovsky Bay on Russia's far east coast.

It is mid-August 2011, and after two gray days, the sun has finally come out. The peninsula that hides the bay looms large and distant. Their home in Vladivostok, 143 miles away, seems like another world.

"I'm going swimming by myself," Denis, a computer programmer, finally announces, setting the guitar aside. Tall, dark and serious, he has dimples that surprise because he smiles so rarely. He flexes his fingers, strong and calloused from plucking guitar strings, and gets up.

Polina, a 25-year-old accountant with long dark hair and a gentle manner, protests. "Please, wait for me," she says. "I want to go too, and I can't see without my glasses!"

Denis, also 25, agrees. He knows that she's nervous about brushing against spiny sea urchins or cutting herself on the sharp rocks in the water. So they set out, one behind the other, swimming toward the tip of a narrow spit about 200 yards from shore known locally as Yearning Heart Island. He leads with a strong breast stroke, frog-kicking and arcing his arms through the water.

At the island, they dive, splash and finally lie in the setting sun to dry off. They stay about 30 minutes, until just before 7 p.m., when it starts to get chilly. For the swim back to camp, Denis again starts out first, straining to see ahead of him in the deep water.

All of a sudden, a shadow about 10 feet long rushes toward him. He turns to the figure, then feels something sink its teeth into his right hand.

"Swim fast to shore, Polina! Go!" he cries. "Shark!"

"What are you talking about?" she asks in disbelief. There are no sharks here.

Then she sees her husband of eight months disappear underwater.

It takes Denis several seconds to realize that the shark is pulling him to the bottom. Below the surface, the water is much colder, and the current is strong. There is a rushing noise in his ears.

Don't take in water, he tells himself fiercely. *Get to the surface. Breathe.*

The shark's sharp teeth are clamped down on his right wrist, and the fish shakes its head back and forth, trying to bite through sinew, muscle and bone.

Without her glasses, Polina can barely make out what's happening. She swims toward Denis's thrashing. And then something with a smooth back and large fin pushes her away. She can make out a shape: the head of her husband coming to the surface once, twice, three times.

"Help!" she screams. "Shark!"

And she starts to swim for her life—and for her husband's. She's not sure if she's swimming toward him or away. All she knows is that she has to get help. "Denis is not going to be your meal. Not today," she says fiercely. Only she is speaking to empty water.

Suddenly, the shark drags Denis back up to the surface. He gulps air before being dragged down again. And again: up and down, back and forth. It's a deadly underwater waltz, with the shark leading the way. Denis fixes on the shark's eyes as it continues to tear at his nearly severed right hand. And then it is gone, along with his wedding ring.

So this is what my death looks like, he tells himself. In a strange way, he feels relieved. People always wonder how they will die, and now he knows.

Then comes a wave of white-hot anger. *I don't want to die. Not today. Not for a long time.*

Punch the shark in the nose.

There it is—an insistent whisper in the back of his mind. He doesn't know where it came from. Maybe he read it once in a book.

Punch the shark? Am I crazy?

But he has nothing to lose. Besides, the shark's snout is right in front of him. He balls his left hand into a fist, hauls back and lets loose. He feels the impact, bone against the shark's nose cartilage.

The shark seems to be angrier and attacks again, this time sinking its teeth into his left wrist. The deadly waltz starts again. Denis is thrashed back and forth until suddenly, the shark lets him go. His left hand is now gone, and his left hip throbs from the six-inch-wide chunk the shark took when Denis tried to get away.

Now Denis just floats in the water, waiting for the shark to come back.

✳   ✳   ✳

Kirill Zenkov and Sergey Torokhov, who are staying at a busier campsite the next beach over, are leaving the bay after loading firewood into Kirill's boat. As Kirill carefully guides the 13-foot-long rubber dinghy through the rocky shoals along the shore, they hear a cry.

"Shh, cut the engine," Sergey, a 33-year-old economist, tells his friend.

Kirill, 35, a sugar salesman, lets the boat idle. They can make out only the word *help*, high and panicked.

"She's drowning," Kirill says, starting the boat again and going full-speed ahead. But when they get near, they're surprised: She is still swimming.

Swimming and screaming at the same time. The boat pulls up beside her, and Sergey pulls her into the boat. She's weeping.

"Save him!" Polina gasps, pointing. "Shark!"

Startled, the two men turn to the left and notice that the sea has turned red around them. Then Sergey sees a shark's fin racing through the water and the head of a man moving with it.

There is no thinking, just instinct powered by adrenaline. The man is just a yard away! Turn the boat!

Kirill pulls up beside Denis.

Sergey says, "Give me your hands."

"I don't have any," Denis replies, holding up his stumps.

Sergey reaches into the water, hoists Denis, bleeding and naked, by his armpits and settles him in Polina's lap, instructing her to hold up the stumps to stem the flow of blood. She does what she's told, even though she can't stand the sight of blood. She rocks her husband and murmurs, "It will be OK. I love you. It will be OK."

Denis is white from loss of blood, but he refuses to close his eyes. He's scared he might never open them again.

Denis is white from loss of blood, but he refuses to close his eyes. He's scared he might never open them again.

As he guns the engine, Kirill sees the shark's huge shadow moving beneath the boat. There's no time to think about being tipped over. It takes seven minutes to get around the peninsula and back to the bay. When they lift Denis out of the boat, people on the beach fall silent. Even now, Denis is shy about his nakedness and asks them to cover him up. Someone brings a towel. Others rifle through first aid kits, looking for antiseptic ointment, hydrogen peroxide and bandages. Kirill calls the police and an ambulance.

"We need a helicopter. There's been a shark attack," he begins.

But the man at the other end of the line is dismissive. "You're drunk. There are no sharks in that area," he says.

Kirill just hangs up. He doesn't have time to argue. Both his parents are doctors, and he knows Denis must get to a hospital immediately.

The two men tie off Denis's arms as best they can with tent rope, cover the backseat of Sergey's Land Cruiser with canvas and set off for the hospital, about 40 miles away. Polina sits in the back, too, talking with Denis to keep him conscious.

It's a bumpy race against death, much of it on a single-lane, unpaved road. Sergey shaves the driving time in half, making the first village in 40 minutes. By then, Kirill, who has a mobile phone pasted to each ear, knows they are looking for an ambulance that has been sent from Slavyanka. They meet up with it and follow it to the hospital.

* * *

The next afternoon, Polina takes a deep breath before walking into the hospital room to see her husband for the first time since she left him the night before as he was being rushed into surgery. *He looks so tiny in his bed, surrounded by machines*, she thinks.

What remains of his arms is hidden under swaths of bandages. Then he smiles, showing his dimples.

"I'm so happy nothing happened to you," he says.

She wants to hold him tight. "The danger has passed," she whispers. "Everything is going to be OK."

Funded by well-wishers, Denis travels to South Korea and Germany for skin grafts to his hip and physiotherapy to adapt to his new prosthetic hands. He and Polina, both now 27, move to Sakhalin Island, off the eastern coast of Russia, where he went to school, and he starts work again as a programmer. He has taken up playing the drums, trying to find a rhythm to a life that nearly wasn't. Sometimes he misses a beat. But he is grateful that he has the chance to try again.

2. THE BOY UNDER A SAND DUNE

The two little boys follow their fathers up the sand dune, scrambling under and through a little cable fence that marks the path. Minutes ago, they were down on the beach enjoying a July afternoon on Lake Michigan. But this is the Indiana Dunes National Lakeshore, the two families are on vacation together, and the big draw is the massive, barren sand dunes that the waves and winds have deposited on the Great Lake's eastern shore. Beckoning most strongly is the steep, impressive, 126-foot Mount Baldy, just a stone's throw from the beach. Greg Woessner and his 6-year-old son, Nathan, have decided on an impromptu ramble with Keith Karrow and his little boy Colin, age 7, family friends. Leaving siblings and spouses on the beach, they frolic their way toward the summit. Then, a little more than halfway up, Nathan vanishes.

Colin hollers ahead to the fathers. "Nathan fell!"

The men whirl around. Nathan is gone. A moment of befuddlement, mixed with a rising panic. "He fell in this hole," Colin says.

There is, in fact, a hole, as smooth as a bore but not even 18 inches across. Greg kneels and calls out to his son, and Nathan answers from somewhere down in that dark: "I'm scared!"

They can't see him. They dangle their arms down into the hole and feel only emptiness. *What is this? What has just happened?* Greg stands and looks around, for a rope, a stick, anything to reach his son. There is nothing but sand. So he kneels again and starts digging with his bare hands. Keith joins in, a frantic pawing at the loose sand. "We're going to get you out," Greg says. And then the hole collapses in on itself, the sugar sand rushing to smooth and fill the temporary interruption of the dune's perfect contour. It is as if the hole and the boy had never been.

Nathan's mother, Faith Woessner, can't quite understand what Colin has run across the beach to tell her, but it's clear that Nathan is in danger, so she sprints the couple of hundred yards up the side of Mount Baldy until she can see Keith kneeling and digging at the sand and Greg walking downhill toward her with a stricken look. "Nathan has fallen," he says. "We can't find him. He's under the sand." She runs to the depression they've been working at and starts gouging at the sand. The three of them dig furiously, excruciatingly aware of the seconds ticking away. "Lord, please give him an air pocket," Faith prays. "Please help my little boy to breathe. Please help us find him."

But seconds turn to minutes, and the digging is the stuff of nightmares: Each time they gain some depth, sand rushes down from uphill, undoing the better part of their efforts. Still they dig. Keith's wife, Rachel, has called 911, and as the minutes drag by, first responders appear on the hillside—police, firefighters, EMTs, none of them carrying a shovel. They, too, kneel and dig. Faith is still praying; the hole keeps filling back in. Radios crackle: tools, backup, excavators. An hour has gone by.

More firefighters show up, with shovels. The site now crawls with some

The Michigan City rescue team as they dig for Nathan; Nathan, celebrating his sixth birthday.

40 people, all desperate to move sand, but even with the tools, at the end of another hour, they have achieved only 5 feet of depth, with no sign of Nathan. No one will state the obvious, but everyone knows that you do not survive burial in sand for 2 hours: They are looking for a body. But streaked with sweat and sand, Faith stands beside the hole, the same prayer on her lips: "Give him an air pocket. Let him breathe. Hold him in your arms. Help us find him."

An excavator appears at the bottom of the dune. They watch its tires wallow, see the driver struggle to coax the machine uphill, and, with a desperate feeling, watch it turn back and disappear down the beach. They dig. Faith goes on praying. Another machine appears, a tracked backhoe, and its driver performs utter gymnastics using its arms to pull itself up the slope. But when it arrives, Faith is terrified. "They'll cut him in half," she tells Greg.

A firefighter is using a rod to probe the sand before the backhoe operator carefully scrapes away 2 inches at a time. Two larger machines labor up the hill and start pulling the sand aside. News helicopters hang in the sky; out over the lake, the sun reddens and dips. Greg and Faith are ushered down off the hill and taken to the police station, where they sit in their swimwear numbly answering questions about the loss of their boy.

*   *   *

The man working the probe hits an object a few inches down and they paw at the sand, certain they've found Nathan, but as they dig, he seems to sink away. More probing; more excavator work. Again, they believe they've found something. This time, sure enough, a firefighter scoops away a layer of sand to reveal the top of the little boy's blond head. He is positioned upright in the dune and has been underground for about 4 hours; an excavator operator estimates the depth at 23 feet. Gingerly they uncover the body as far down as the armpits, and the firefighter lifts it out, fighting back a swell of grief, overwhelmed by the resemblance to his own little boy. He wipes the sand from the lifeless face and passes the child up and out of the hole. No heartbeat. No breath. Ice cold. His colleagues drape a tarp over their heads so the news cameras won't record the grisly scene of Nathan's little body being carried down the hillside. The sun finishes its setting in a spectacular display over the lake.

More probing; more excavator work. Again, they believe they've found something.

At the police station, an officer tells Greg and Faith that their son has been found but won't tell them if he's alive or dead. The two rush to the hospital and sit in a waiting area until an EMT enters. They don't hear most of what he says, because they are stopped short by the first two words: *He's alive.* The rest of it they'll piece together later: how, on the way down the beach in the bed of a lifeguard truck, the seemingly lifeless boy who had been buried under 20 feet of sand suddenly began to bleed from a small cut on his face, evidence of a beating heart; how there must have been an air pocket; how the cold sand at that depth must have so cooled his body as to reduce demand for oxygen. Still later, they will learn that the hole was likely the vestigial impression of a rotted-out tree, long since consumed by the ever-moving dune.

And Nathan's recovery proves no less miraculous than his survival. Doctors suction sand from his mouth, his trachea, his lungs; he regains consciousness, begins to speak. Within two weeks, he is home playing with his siblings. The brain damage half-expected by the professionals never appears, although Nathan remembers nothing about his ordeal. The impossibility of it is vexing, but not to the aptly named Faith, who has her own explanation: "God did this for us. He really does answer prayers. This is God's miracle."

3. CAUGHT IN A RIPTIDE

It's a well-conceived first date for lifelong surfer Chase Newsom and scuba dive master Cynthia Hatfield: The two Southern Californians will spend an afternoon honing Cynthia's novice surfing skills on the waters of Orange County's Aliso Beach. Unfortunately, their Saturday afternoon date comes on the heels of the worst Pacific storm to hit the area in years, and by the time they put on their wet suits, the water is too rough. The surfing lesson is out of the question.

The two agree to splash around in the shallow water just a few feet from shore instead. But within seconds, they realize their mistake. An 8-foot wave comes in with startling force. Chase, the surfer, lets the water push him toward shore, where he stands and collects himself. But when Cynthia, the diver, negotiates the wave by ducking under it, she is shocked by the strength of its pull away from shore, diagonal from the beach. She gets her bearings and starts to wade toward land, when a second wave hits.

Cynthia tries ducking again, but this wave slams even harder. She knows she can hold her breath for about a minute, and as she feels the seconds ticking away, she begins to wonder if she'll surface before her time is up. She does, and she finds her footing and calls to Chase, who is alarmingly far away now. She's been pulled both down the beach and out to sea. "I think I want to get out," she yells. She looks around just in time to see a third wave towering over her. There's no time to duck this one, and it sends her spinning underwater, where once again she tests the limits of her breath. When at last she begins to see sunlight through her clenched eyelids and bobs to the surface for air, she has been pulled a quarter mile from shore.

The waves are enormous. They're not breaking, though, and she can stroke without getting pounded. But the water temperature is in the 50s. She can't stay out here forever.

*   *   *

Swimming to shore is out of the question. For one thing, although she's strong, she doesn't know if she'll survive another encounter with the surf break. And the current has pulled her down shore from Aliso Beach; to her eye, she'll come ashore in the next cove, which is studded with rocks and reefs. She knows that getting slammed by a wave into a barnacle-covered reef would cut her to shreds, maybe even crack her skull. With no good options, Cynthia marks time, paddling seaward to avoid the suck of the waves that keep trying to draw her toward the surf line.

Chase is astounded by how quickly Cynthia has been pulled away. An Orange County Lifeguards truck rolls onto the beach, and he runs over to where the rescuer is pulling on his wet suit and fins. "My friend is out there," Chase says.

"OK," the lifeguard replies. "I'm going out there."

A powerful storm roils waters along the Southern California coast on March 2, 2014.

"Do you want me to paddle out and get her?" Chase asks, but the lifeguard doesn't respond. Chase shrugs and runs back to the beach, determined to try. To his surprise, someone else is already swimming through the surf toward Cynthia.

Chase flings himself onto his surfboard and begins paddling furiously. He makes it past the break before the waves begin crashing again. He doesn't know what he'll do once he gets to Cynthia besides help her stay afloat and commiserate.

The swimmer beats Chase to Cynthia and introduces himself as Brennan, a former local lifeguard. "Are you OK?" he asks.

"I'm fine," Cynthia answers. "I'm so sorry you had to come out here. I was sucked out really quickly."

After a few minutes, Chase paddles up and shares his surfboard with her. The trio is quickly joined by the local lifeguard Chase had spoken to on the beach and two Laguna Beach guards, who were responding to a 911 call a bystander had made. The Laguna Beach rescuers, Matt Grace and Casey Parlette, determine that the best option is to ride the current while they wait for a rescue boat. It is no casual treading of water; they need to be close enough that they can make a break for shore if necessary, but not so close that the waves suck them back into the surf. They fall into an endless pattern of paddling hard out to sea, getting pulled in by the nearly 15-foot waves, and paddling hard seaward again. For an hour, they rise and fall together in the cold water, counting the waves, timing the breakers. The sets are too close together for them to risk an attempt to the shore.

Suddenly, a wave that looks the size of an apartment complex mounts. "Swim!"

"I'll go back," the Orange County lifeguard finally says. "I'll brief them on the situation."

The group watches him depart. Cynthia, who is connected to both Laguna Beach guards by a rescue tube with a tether, can see that an ambulance has arrived on the scene, and EMTs are unloading stretchers. *Please let there be a boat*, she thinks.

Suddenly, a wave that looks the size of an apartment complex mounts. The Laguna Beach guards yell, "Swim!" Matt, who is farthest from shore, fins hard, managing to make the crest, but now he is on the back side of the wave, while Cynthia and Casey—still tethered to Matt—are on the front. Casey disconnects himself from the rig, seizes Cynthia, and pushes her into the tube as Matt spread-eagles his body to create enough drag to keep Cynthia from being carried off. There is a mad yank on the tether, and then Casey and Cynthia burst through to the back of the wave, gasping.

"Keep swimming!" Matt yells, and Cynthia sees another stupendous wave. The timing of this one is worse; Cynthia knows that the rescue tube will catch its full force. Casey slips the tube over her head and wraps his arms around her, and they kick hard to slice into the wave. It feels like half a minute of frenzied kicking before they break through.

"Don't stop swimming," Casey says.

A few more seconds of effort and they're clear of the break, but now they notice another lifeguard battling his way out through the surf to reach them. When he arrives, he tells the group what they already know: They should not try to swim in—a boat is on its way. They've been in the water for nearly 2 hours.

Finally, a boat arrives, and the Orange County Harbor Patrol plucks the swimmers from the water and carries them to its basin at Dana Point Harbor. The group is cold and exhausted, but no one is seriously injured.

Cynthia regrets that she put herself in the situation, but she is grateful for the lifeguards' bravery and professionalism. "I knew if I did what you said, I'd be fine," she tells them as the boat motors into the harbor. "I knew I was in good hands."

Originally published in August 2014 issue of *Reader's Digest* magazine.

My ultimate goal in life
is to read books I like,
listen to music I enjoy,
play with my cats,
drink some semi-decent
red wine and watch
a live baseball game
on TV. Living itself is
adventure enough.

—HARUKI MURAKAMI,
Novelist in *Interview Magazine*

Humor Hall of Fame

My dad joined the Navy out of spite.
He was a petty officer.

—FORCES.NET

At the outpatient surgery center where I work, the anesthesiologist chats with patients before their operations to help them relax. One day, he thought he recognized a woman as a coworker from the VA hospital where he had trained. When the patient confirmed that his hunch was correct, the anesthesiologist said, "So tell me, is the food there still as bad as it used to be?"

"I suppose," she replied. "I'm still cooking it."

—GCFL.NET

Our boatswain's mate was a smoker who would toss his matches overboard. Then one day, he surprised us all when he popped a cigarette in his mouth and produced an expensive lighter from his pocket. With great fanfare, he flipped open the top, flicked the spark wheel, lit his cigarette ... then chucked the lighter overboard.

—BOB MCCORD

"When did 'At ease' become 'Chill'?"

You have to use your voice, even if it shakes. There are times when you will ask for change, and there are times when you'll create it.

—ALLYSON FELIX,
Sprinter, to graduates of the
University of Southern California

—And Sudden Death

by J.C. Furnas

One of the most widely read articles of its time, with its grisly detail of the carnage on our highways, hopefully it will still shock readers into better driving habits

L̲ike the gruesome spectacle of a bad automobile accident itself, the realistic details of this article will nauseate some readers. Those who find themselves thus affected at the outset are cautioned against reading the article in its entirety, since there is no letdown in the author's outspoken treatment of sickening facts.

Publicizing the total of motoring injuries—almost a million last year, with 36,000 deaths—never gets to first base in jarring the motorist into a realization of the appalling risks of motoring. He does not translate dry statistics into a reality of blood and agony.

Figures exclude the pain and horror of savage mutilation—which means they leave out the point. They need to be brought closer home. A passing look at a bad smash or the news that a fellow you had lunch with last week is in a hospital with a broken back will make any driver but a born fool slow down at least temporarily. But what is needed is a vivid and *sustained* realization that every time you step on the throttle, death gets in beside you, hopefully waiting for his chance. That single horrible accident you may have witnessed is no isolated horror. That sort of thing happens every hour of the day, everywhere in the United States. If you really felt *that*, perhaps the stickful of type in Monday's paper recording that a total of 29 local citizens were killed in weekend crashes would rate something more than a perfunctory tut-tut as you turn back to the sports page.

An enterprising judge now and again sentences reckless drivers to tour the accident end of a city morgue. But even a mangled body on a slab, waxily portraying the consequences of bad motoring judgment, isn't a patch on the scene of the accident itself. No artist working on a safety poster would dare depict that in full detail.

That picture would have to include motion picture and sound effects too—the flopping, pointless efforts of the injured to stand up; the queer, grunting noises; the steady, panting groaning of a human being with pain creeping up on him as the shock wears off. It should portray the slack expression on the face of a man, drugged with shock, staring at the Z-twist in his broken leg, the insane crumpled effect of a child's body after its bones are crushed inward, a realistic portrait of a hysterical woman with her screaming mouth opening a hole in the bloody drip that fills her eyes and runs off her chin. Minor details would include the raw ends of bones protruding through flesh in compound fractures, and the dark red, oozing surfaces where clothes and skin were flayed off at once.

Those are all standard, everyday sequels to the modern passion for going places in a hurry and taking a chance or two by the way. If ghosts could be put to a useful purpose, every bad stretch of road in the United States would greet the oncoming motorist with groans and screams and the educational spectacle of 10 or a dozen corpses, all sizes, sexes and ages, lying horribly still on the bloody grass.

The car was all folded up like an accordion—the color was about all there was left.

Last year a state trooper of my acquaintance stopped a big man for speeding. Papa was obviously a responsible person, obviously set for a pleasant weekend with his family—so the officer cut into papa's well-bred expostulations: "I'll let you off this time, but if you keep on this way, you won't last long. Get going—but take it easier." Later a passing motorist hailed the trooper and asked if the big man had got a ticket. "No," said the trooper, "I hated to spoil their party." "Too bad you didn't," said the motorist, "I saw you stop them—and then I passed that car again 50 miles up the line. It still makes me feel sick at my stomach. The car was all folded up like an accordion—the color was about all there was left. They were all dead but one of the kids—and he wasn't going to live to the hospital."

It's like going over Niagara Falls in a steel barrel full of railroad spikes.

Maybe it will make you sick at your stomach too. But unless you're a heavy-footed incurable, a good look at the picture the artist wouldn't dare paint, a firsthand acquaintance with the results of mixing gasoline with speed and bad judgment, ought to be well worth your while. I can't help it if the facts are revolting. If you have the nerve to drive fast and take chances, you ought to have the nerve to take the appropriate cure. You can't ride an ambulance or watch the doctor working on the victim in the hospital, but you can read.

The automobile is treacherous, just as a cat is. It is tragically difficult to realize that it can become the deadliest missile. As enthusiasts tell you, it makes 65 feel like nothing at all. But 65 an hour is 100 feet a second, a speed which puts a viciously unjustified responsibility on brakes and human reflexes, and can instantly turn this docile luxury into a mad bull elephant.

Collision, turnover or sideswipe, each type of accident produces either a shattering dead stop or a crashing change of direction—and, since the occupant—meaning you—continues in the old direction at the original speed, every surface and angle of the car's interior immediately becomes a battering, tearing projectile, aimed squarely at you—inescapable. There is no bracing yourself against these imperative laws of momentum.

It's like going over Niagara Falls in a steel barrel full of railroad spikes. The best thing that can happen to you—and one of the rarer things—is to be thrown out as the doors spring open, so you have only the ground to reckon with. You are spared the lethal array of gleaming metal knobs and edges and glass inside the car.

Anything can happen in that split second of crash, even those lucky escapes you hear about. People have dived through windshields and come out with only superficial scratches. They have run cars together head-on, reducing both to twisted junk, and been found unhurt and arguing bitterly two minutes afterward. But death was there just the same—he was only exercising his privilege of being erratic. In spring a wrecking crew pried

Bodies are often found with their shoes off and their feet all broken out of shape.

the door off a car which had been overturned down an embankment and out stepped the driver with only a scratch on his cheek. But his mother was still inside, a splinter of wood from the top driven four inches into her brain as a result of son's taking a greasy curve a little too fast. No blood—no horribly twisted bones—just a gray-haired corpse still clutching her pocketbook in her lap as she had clutched it when she felt the car leave the road.

On that same curve a month later, a light touring car crashed a tree. In the middle of the front seat they found a nine-month-old baby surrounded by broken glass and yet absolutely unhurt. A fine practical joke on death—but spoiled by the baby's parents, still sitting on each side of him, instantly killed by shattering their skulls on the dashboard.

If you customarily pass without clear vision a long way ahead, make sure that every member of the party carries identification papers—it's difficult to identify a body with its whole face bashed in or torn off. The driver is death's favorite target. If the steering wheel holds together it ruptures his liver or spleen so he bleeds to death internally. Or, if the steering wheel breaks off, the matter is settled instantly by the steering column's plunging through his abdomen.

By no means do all head-on collisions occur on curves. The modern deathtrap is likely to be a straight stretch with three lanes of traffic—like the notorious Astor Flats on the Albany Post Road where there have been as many as 27 fatalities in one summer month. This sudden vision of broad, straight road tempts many an ordinarily sensible driver into passing the man ahead. Simultaneously, a driver coming the other way swings out at high speed. At the last moment each tries to get into line again, but the gaps are closed. As the cars in line are forced into the ditch to capsize or crash fences, the passers meet, almost head-on, in a swirling, grinding smash that sends them caroming obliquely into the others.

A trooper described such an accident—five cars in one mess, seven killed on the spot, two dead on the way to the hospital, two more dead in the long run. He remembered it far more vividly than he wanted to—the quick way the doctor turned away from a dead man to check up on a woman with a broken back; the three bodies out of one car so soaked with oil from the crankcase that they looked like wet brown cigars and not human at all: a man, walking around and babbling to himself, oblivious of the dead and dying, even oblivious of the dagger-like sliver of steel that stuck out of his streaming wrist; a pretty girl with her forehead laid open, trying hopelessly to crawl out of a ditch in spite of her smashed hip. A first-class massacre of that sort is only a question of scale and numbers—seven corpses are no deader than one. Each shattered man, woman or child who went to make up the 36,000 corpses chalked up last year had to die a personal death.

A car careening and rolling down a bank, battering and smashing its occupants every inch of the way, can wrap itself so thoroughly around a tree that front and rear bumpers interlock, requiring an acetylene torch to cut them apart. In a recent case of that sort they found the old lady, who had been sitting in back, lying across the lap of her daughter, who was in front, each soaked in her own and the other's blood indistinguishably, each so shattered and broken that there was no point whatever in an autopsy to determine whether it was broken neck or ruptured heart that caused death.

Overturning cars specialize in certain injuries.

Overturning cars specialize in certain injuries. Cracked pelvis, for instance, guaranteeing agonizing months in bed, motionless, perhaps crippled for life—broken spine resulting from sheer sidewise twist—the minor details of smashed knees and splintered shoulder blades caused by crashing into the side of the car as she goes over with the swirl of an insane roller coaster—and the lethal consequences of broken ribs, which puncture hearts and lungs with their raw ends. The consequent internal hemorrhage is no less dangerous because it is the pleural instead of the abdominal cavity that is filling with blood.

Flying glass contributes much more than its share to the spectacular side of accidents. It doesn't merely cut—the fragments are driven in as if a cannon loaded with broken bottles had been fired in your face, and a sliver in the eye, traveling with such force, means certain blindness. A leg or arm stuck through the windshield will cut clean to the bone through vein, artery and muscle like a piece of beef under the butcher's knife, and it takes little time to lose a fatal amount of blood under such circumstances. Even safety glass may not be wholly safe when the car crashes something at high speed. You hear picturesque tales of how a flying human body will make a neat hole in the stuff with its head—the shoulders stick—the glass holds—and the raw, keen edge of the hole decapitates the body as neatly as a guillotine.

Or, to continue with the decapitation motif, going off the road into a post-and-rail fence can put you beyond worrying about other injuries immediately when a rail comes through the windshield and tears off your head with its splintery end—not as neat a job but thoroughly efficient. Bodies are often found with their shoes off and their feet all broken out of shape. The shoes are back on the floor of the car, empty and with their laces still neatly tied. That is the kind of impact produced by modern speeds.

But all that is routine in every American community. To be remembered individually by doctors and policemen, you have to do something as grotesque as the lady who burst the windshield with her head, splashing splinters all over the other occupants of the car, and then, as the car rolled over, rolled with it down the edge of the windshield frame and cut her throat from ear to ear. Or park on the pavement too near a curve at night and stand in front of the taillight as you take off the spare tire—which will immortalize you in somebody's memory as the fellow who was mashed three feet broad and two inches thick by the impact of a heavy-duty truck against the rear of his own car. Or be as original as the pair of youths who were thrown out of an open roadster in spring—thrown clear—but each broke a windshield post with his head in passing and the whole top of each skull, down to the eyebrows, was missing. Or snap off a nine-inch tree and get yourself impaled by a ragged branch.

None of all that is scare-fiction; it is just the horrible raw material of the year's statistics as seen in the ordinary course of duty by policemen and doctors, picked at random. The surprising thing is that there is so little dissimilarity in the stories they tell.

It's hard to find a surviving accident victim who can bear to talk. After you come to, the gnawing, searing pain throughout your body is accounted for by learning that you have both collarbones smashed, both shoulder blades splintered, your right arm broken in three places and three ribs cracked, with every chance of bad internal ruptures. But the pain can't distract you, as the shock begins to wear off, from realizing that you are probably on your way out. You can't forget that, not even when they shift you from the ground to the stretcher and your broken ribs bite into your lungs and the sharp ends of your collarbones slide over to stab deep into each side of your screaming throat. When you've stopped screaming, it all comes back—you're dying and you hate yourself for it. That isn't fiction either. It's what it actually feels like to be one of that 36,000.

When you've stopped screaming, it all comes back—you're dying and you hate yourself for it. That isn't fiction either.

And every time you pass on a blind curve, every time you hit it up on a slippery road, every time you step on it harder than your reflexes will safely take, every time you drive with your reactions slowed down by a drink or two, every time you follow the man ahead too closely, you're gambling a few seconds against this kind of blood and agony and sudden death.

Take a look at yourself as the man in the white jacket shakes his head over you, tells the boys with the stretcher not to bother and turns away to somebody else who isn't quite dead yet. And then take it easy.

Originally published in August 1935 issue of *Reader's Digest* magazine.

After Reader's Digest *co-founder DeWitt Wallace got in a car accident, he sent J.C. Furnas to talk with police and highway patrolmen to get reports of accident scenes. The article that ran was a blockbuster.*

As per another Reader's Digest *article by Charles Ferguson: "For all its guts and gore, it had dignity. Five thousand proofs of '—And Sudden Death' were sent out to newspapers and other publications, with permission to reprint ... It ran in newspapers in every large U.S. city and in many other publications. It was read and discussed on radio, in schools, churches, lunch clubs. The demand for reprints of the article would continue for two decades. It was without doubt the most widely read article ever published at that time."*

WHO'S ON FIRST?

Trying to keep my Little Leaguers settled in the dugout was quite the task. I explained that the next batter up is called "on deck." The batter after that is "in the hole." If they weren't on deck or in the hole, they had to sit down. One player kept asking what the batter after "in the hole" is called. I kept saying there was no name for that. He called those batters "IN THE WAY!" It was so funny, and that's what we called it for the rest of the season.

—Cheryl Stetz Bamert, *Parsippany, NJ*

A SWING AND A MISS

I played on a softball team with many rookies who'd never played before. One of my teammates hit a hard line drive. As she rounded first, we hollered, "Go to third!" And so she did—right across the pitcher's mound.

—Gail Valence, *Henrietta, NY*

My Hut

by Cathrin Bradbury from the *Toronto Star*

A backyard sanctuary promised solitude—
until I realized that I didn't want to be alone

My first reaction when my son told me last summer I was going to be a grandmother, and that the baby and his parents would live with me, was unbounded joy. My second reaction was to build a 10x10 wooden hut in my backyard. It comes with a silver key that is mine alone.

My son, Kelly, and his partner, Vonnie, moved in a few months later, in between relocating to Toronto from Guatemala and saving up for their dream apartment. Meanwhile, we all fit in the white stucco two-story family home in midtown Toronto, eat mostly healthy meals—sometimes together, sometimes not, no pressure—and share a copacetic, early-to-bed-and-rise schedule.

With a full house, however, I now work where I sleep. The surprise baby news was when my gaze turned to the potential of the old tool shed at the back of our haphazard yard. Where others saw a teardown, I saw a magical portal to another world. A place, after a modest fix-up with a few nails and a hammer, to write and explore an unabashedly interior life, just a few footsteps away.

One of the things about building a hut is that it requires a lot of decisions. The mind twister is that you need a hut, and the room it provides for contemplation, to decide whether you need a hut. In this period of decision making, which lasted about six weeks, people would say words to me, and I would wonder how long good manners decreed before I could steer the conversation to my hut. (About a minute was where I generally landed.) Existing shed or new prefab (the latter, in the end); facing garden or house (garden); roof angle (sloping down to the north); wiring complexities; heating. A hut needs a cement slab, which involves soil disposal bins, a cement mixer and a four-person work crew.

"Doing a lot of these huts, I hear," I said to the cement boss.

"These what?"

"Huts. You know. What we're building."

"I wouldn't know anything about that," he said, smoothing the fresh cement in broad sweeps with his pallet. "We call these shed slabs."

A hut is not a house.

This is the kind of profound thinking that comes from working inside my now finished hut.

In footsteps, this gleaming spruce-wood structure is 33 small steps from my back door. But in all other ways my daily journey to the end of the back-yard can't be measured in something as unremarkable as putting one foot in front of the other while holding a mug of coffee, the key that unlocks the hut door and a woolen blanket, because it gets chilly out here sometimes.

There are the sounds, to begin there. From the house, the noises are of cars and ambulances and boots over ice and snow. Back here, it's rain, sleet and wind, except it's like the weather is happening inside the thin walls of the hut, not outside. It can be worrying, but it keeps you alert. The birds' songs are nice; the manic squirrels trying to dig through the roof—they seem affronted by my presence—less so.

In a hut, the only movement is of your own thoughts.

The other thing about a hut that is nothing like a house (or an apartment, or anywhere people live) is that a house has momentum. People arrive and leave, things are dropped off at the door, mail is delivered, garbage is taken away. In a hut, the only movement is of your own thoughts. That the word "hut" was taken over by marketing to mean something welcoming and fun—Pizza Hut! Sunglass Hut!—is a misdirection. Hut comes from the old English *hydan*, to hide, cover or conceal. The plot twist is that a hut is less a place to hide out in, or to give the slip to prospective grandchildren, than it is a place to find what is hidden from you.

I think about my grandchild-to-be—a recurring hut fantasy is him running to the end of the path and knocking on the hut door; yes, he knocks, he is a polite child—and the risk of new love. And whether I can protect him from the dangerous world, and how this hut is going to be too cold for him in the winter and I'd better get more blankets.

As day darkens into evening, Kelly and Vonnie come down from working upstairs in their own offices, and then the kitchen at the back of the house is suddenly ablaze with light. It's one of the best parts of my day, when those lights come on. It's when I understand that the hut, and my retreat to it, is made warmer by the light that comes from the house.

I quickly turn off the hut's heat and lights, gather up my mug, key and blanket, and walk the 33 steps back to the house. Kelly is the house cook; Vonnie and I the sous-chefs. Kelly hands me a head of cabbage for the fish tacos, explaining how he wants it. "Thinly sliced. Not chopped."

"So, Mom," he says after a bit, looking sadly down at my unevenly sliced cabbage. "We're thinking we're going to maybe keep our eyes open for an apartment nearby."

"An apartment? But how will the baby get to my hut?" I was shaken as much by the idea of them moving as by the ancient wobbly timbre of my voice. I sounded like one of the hysterical fathers in a Jane Austen novel when his daughter announces her plans to move a few hundred meters across the flowering meadow to live with her new husband.

"You know, a place of our own," said Kelly.

"Ah," I said. "Right. Of course."

I can't think what it'll be like when they're gone. If their light doesn't shine on my hut at the end of the day, does the hut even exist? Or, if it does exist, should it? It's too big a thought to grapple with as we assemble the fish tacos.

I'll think about it on Monday. In the hut.

Originally published in October 2022 *Reader's Digest* international editions.

Humor Hall of Fame

My 4-year-old is singing a song she made up. The only words are "Everything's a mess and I don't care." It's the song of our time.

—@XPLODINGUNICORN

My 3-year-old daughter stuck out her hand and said, "Look at the fly I killed, Mommy." Since she was eating a juicy pickle at the time, I thrust her contaminated hands under the faucet and washed them with antibacterial soap. After sitting her down to finish her pickle, I asked, with a touch of awe, "How did you kill that fly all by yourself?" Between bites, she said, "I hit it with my pickle."

—CINDY YATES

We recently brought our 4-year-old daughter along to a doctor's appointment for my wife, who is expecting. The doctor placed a monitor on my wife's stomach, and we could hear the sound of a heartbeat. "That's your little brother," I told our daughter. "I know!" she replied. "Those are his footsteps."

—TOM ALBIG

Conan

"Greetings, diary."

WHAT DOES A LIAR LOOK LIKE? "It is always the best policy to tell the truth, unless, of course, you are an exceptionally good liar," humorist Jerome K. Jerome wrote about 100 years ago. Exceptionally good liars know they shouldn't avert their eyes when telling a fib. They know that's a telltale sign that honest people look for. (Who hasn't heard the old canard "Liars never look you in the eye"?)

Liar, Liar

by Andy Simmons

When faced with evidence of blatant wrongdoing, some people take a deep breath, put their hands on the Bible, and ... deny, deny, deny!

"Of course I complete the Saturday *New York Times* crossword puzzle ... in pen!"

"I never check out my exes on Facebook."

"No, I don't mind sitting outside the ladies' changing room in Macy's while you try on the entire spring collection."

* * *

Admit it. You lie. And if you say you don't, you're a liar. We all lie, as often as two or three times every 10 minutes, says one study (if it can be trusted). Sounds pretty reprehensible, right? But consider the alternative.

"You can't stop lies entirely," University of Massachusetts psychologist Robert Feldman told *U.S. News & World Report*. "Society would grind to a halt." That's because most of us fib to spare feelings—ours and others: Too much truth hurts. Case in point: When *Cosmopolitan* asked readers for dates-from-hell stories, a guy named Don revealed the pain he felt when his blind date announced, "Your brother is so hot ... you guys look nothing alike."

But while most of us fib to avoid such hard-heartedness, others lie ...

281

WHAT THE FASHIONABLE CRIMINAL IS WEARING. When Eugene Todie pulled up to the New York–Canada border, guards noticed that he was sporting the latest in criminal haute couture, an ankle monitor. Intrigued, they asked Todie, "What's the occasion?"

The lie. Todie explained that a friend urged him to wear it as a show of solidarity with Lindsay Lohan, who was following a court order and wearing one herself.

Were there any suckers? After a background check showed that Todie was on probation for criminal contempt and not allowed to leave the country, he was arrested and awaited a sentence.

like rugs. Take the Brazilian soccer player who claimed he'd been kidnapped just so he could avoid a fine for being late to practice. He was arrested for falsely reporting a crime.

What was this dolt thinking?

He wasn't, says Cornell University professor Jeff Hancock. Consider this mathematical equation: Desperation + Lack of Time = Idiotic Lie. People like him, says Hancock, "should never again put themselves in the position of having to lie on the spot," for the simple reason that they stink at it. And these fibbers should follow the same advice:

NSF(W)

Several staffers at the National Science Foundation (NSF) in Washington, D.C., were investigated for watching porn on their computers at work. The biggest perpetrator: an executive who'd spent 331 days chatting online with naked women, reported the *Washington Times*. But government money—up to $58,000—was not wasted, insisted the man.

The lie. By clicking on the various porn sites, our executive provided these women with a living. "He explained that these young women were from poor countries and needed to make money to help their parents, and this site helped them do it," an investigator reported.

Were there any suckers? His altruism notwithstanding, the official has since "retired." In light of his actions, the foundation has tightened controls to filter out inappropriate internet addresses.

PORK, THE OTHER BANNED SUBSTANCE

Clenbuterol is a drug used by farmers to keep their animals from getting too chubby. Because athletes don't want to waddle across the finish line, some are tempted to try it, even though the International Olympic Committee has banned its use. But when Tong Wen, China's Olympic judo champion, tested positive for clenbuterol after an event, her coach had an explanation for how it ended up in Tong's system.

The lie. She ate "a lot of pork chops," the coach told the BBC. And that pork was tainted by the clenbuterol.

Were there any suckers? Olympic officials are famously vigilant. Years ago, when track star Dennis Mitchell made the claim that lots of sex and beer were responsible for his high levels of testosterone, the International Association of Athletics Federations banned him from racing for two years. But Tong's blame-the-pig defense panned out, sort of. She was cleared by the Court of Arbitration for Sport due to a technicality: She wasn't present when a backup urine sample was tested. The International Judo Federation blasted the ruling, insisting it would have "a very negative influence" on the sports world.

JUST DESSERTS. An Iowa bar was cited for serving alcohol to a minor, specifically, a vodka-infused Jell-O shot.

The lie. Jell-O shots are not alcoholic beverages, the bar owners insisted. Once they become gelatinous globs, the "shots" are a dessert.

Were there any suckers? In her ruling, the judge, an apparent Jell-O-phile, opined: "While there might be some debate as to whether Jell-O is a food item or a beverage, the Jell-O shots served by the licensee were alcoholic beverages." In other words, the dessert has one thing in common with booze—it'll get you blotto.

DECEIT 101

While running for a seat on the Birmingham, Alabama, Board of Education, 23-year-old Dr. Antwon B. Womack said he'd graduated from West End High School and received a bachelor's degree in elementary education from Alabama A&M. Impressive, except that Womack was 21, didn't have a doctorate, didn't attend college and never graduated from high school. Other than that, he told the *Birmingham News*, he was honest.

The lie. "My campaign is not based on a foundation of lies," he insisted.

The truth. "It's just that the information I provided to the people is false."

The honest-to-God truth. The revelations are "really going to hurt my career."

Were there any suckers? Yes, 117 of them. That's how many people voted for Womack, landing him in fourth place out of five candidates.

A CRASH COURSE IN LYING

When Jayson Williams's Mercedes-Benz SUV crashed in Manhattan, officers found the former basketball star sitting in the passenger seat. When asked by police who'd caused the crash, Williams deflected all blame.

The lie. It wasn't me, he quite simply insisted. "Someone else was driving."

IS IT A DAT OR A COG? Landlord Barry Maher has a strict rule against dogs in his Santa Barbara, California, building. Cats? Fine. Dogs? Nope. So when neighbors complained about a barking dog, Maher called the tenant.

The lie. "Oh, I would never have a dog," she told him.

The bigger lie. "What I have is a special breed of cat."

The whopper. "It's a dog-cat. A mix of a dog and a cat."

Were there any suckers? Almost. "It was so crazy that I actually wondered, is there really such a thing as a dog-cat?" Maher told *realestate.msn.com*. There isn't. So tenant and dog-cat were evicted.

PLANE STUPID. Sergei Berejnoi raced through Denver International Airport trying to catch his SkyWest Airlines flight. Unfortunately, he arrived just after the plane had left the gate with his luggage onboard. With his pleas to bring back the plane falling on deaf ears, he offered the gate agent a not-so-subtle reason for doing as he said.

The lie. "There's a bomb in my suitcase."

Were there any suckers? The aircraft was checked for explosives. When none were found, Berejnoi took a trip of another sort, to the police station. He got put on probation.

Were there any suckers? The fact that witnesses had seen Williams behind the wheel, not to mention the absence of anyone else in the car, led authorities to conclude that he'd switched seats. And yes, alcohol was involved.

Originally published in August 2011 issue of *Reader's Digest* magazine.

CREDITS AND ACKNOWLEDGMENTS

"Trapped!" by Lee Karsian, as told to Albert Rosenfeld; *Reader's Digest*, November 1958

"The Day We Flew the Kites" by Frances Fowler; condensed from *Parents'* magazine, May 1949, © 1949 by The Parents' Institute, Inc.; *Reader's Digest*, July 1949
Photograph on page 12 by H. Armstrong Roberts/Getty Images

"How Honest Are We?" by Ralph Kinney Bennett; *Reader's Digest*, December 1995
Photograph on page 18 by MauMyHaT/Getty Images

"When I Met Caruso" by Elizabeth Bacon Rodewald; *Reader's Digest*, July 1955
Photograph on page 30 by Bettmann/Getty Images

"Your Mom Said *What*?" by Marc Peyser; *Reader's Digest*, May 2019
Illustrations on page 40, 41, 42, 43 and 45 by Edwin Fotheringham

"A Girl, a Seal and the Sea" by Per Ola and Emily D'Aulaire; *Reader's Digest*, September 1994
Photograph on page 48 by JamersonG/Getty Images

"Lost Beneath the Mountain" by Per Ola and Emily D'Aulaire; *Reader's Digest*, July 1992

"The Slave in the Garage" by Mary A. Fischer; *Reader's Digest*, May 2008
Photographs on page 69 photographed by Lori Stoll; on page 70 courtesy of the Irvine Police Dept.; on page 73 by Ana Venegas/The Orange County Register via Southern California News Group

"'I Love You'" by George H. Grant; *Reader's Digest*, May 1962

"In the Jaws of a Polar Bear" by Robert Kiener; *Reader's Digest*, March 2011
Photographs on page 82 by Steven J. Kazlowski/Alamy Stock Photo; on page 85 courtesy of Robert Kiener; on pages 87 and 88 by Ludvig Fjeld

"Best Cheap Fun!" by Mary Roach; *Reader's Digest*, May 2007
Photograph on page 94 by dimarik/Getty Images

"The Price of Freedom" by Ben Montgomery, from *Gangrey.com*, Sept. 21, 2015, © 2015 by Ben Montgomery; *Reader's Digest*, July/August 2017

Photographs on page 99 courtesy Ben Montgomery; on page 100 courtesy Ben Montgomery, Illustration Robert Karr; on page 102 by Hulton-Deutsch Collection/Getty Images; on page 103 courtesy Ben Montgomery

"Goodbye to Shamrock" by Frederic A. Birmingham; *Reader's Digest*, December 1968
Photograph on page 104 by Dmitrii Anikin/Getty Images

"Little Boy Blue of Chester, Nebraska" by Henry Hurt; *Reader's Digest*, December 1987
Photograph on page 110 by Ryan McGinnis/Getty Images

"The Doctor of Lennox" by A.J. Cronin; *Reader's Digest*, September 1939
Illustration on page 120 by powerofforever/Getty Images

"'But We're ALIVE!'" by Doris Agee; *Reader's Digest*, June 1967
Photograph on page 128 by Luís Henrique Boucault/Getty Images

"Three Days of Silence That Saved a Life" by J. Campbell Bruce; *Reader's Digest*, August 1957

"They Volunteered for Cancer" by Ruth and Edward Brecher; *Reader's Digest*, April 1958
    Photograph on page 148 by H. Armstrong Roberts/ ClassicStock/Getty Images

"Why Do I Look So Familiar" by Corey Ford; *Reader's Digest*, August 1964

"The Phantom of the Woods" by Doris Cheney Whitehouse; *Reader's Digest*, March 1960
    Photograph on page 160 by Schon/Getty Images

"The Case of the Murdered Mother-in-Law" by Gerald Moore; *Reader's Digest*, January 1985

"The Day the Atomic Age Was Born" by Herbert L. Anderson, as told to J.D. Ratcliff; *Reader's Digest*, March 1969

"Wandering in the Alaskan Winter" by Brian Murphy,

from *81 Days Below Zero* by Brian Murphy, copyright © 2015. Reprinted by permission of Da Capo Press, an imprint of Hachette Book Group, Inc.; *Reader's Digest*, December/ January 2017-2018
    Illustrations on pages 184, 187 and 188 by Illustrations by Levente Szabo

"Are You Too Boring for Therapy?" by Cassie Barradas; *Reader's Digest* international editions, January/February 2020
    Illustration on page 198 by Steven Twigg

"'There Wasn't Time to Scream'" by Per Ola and Emily D'Aulaire; *Reader's Digest*, July 1982
    Photograph on page 200 by Bettmann Archive/Getty Images

"She Rode to Triumph Over Polio" by Edwin Muller; *Reader's Digest*, August 1955
    Photograph on page 212 by Keystone-France/Getty Images

"'I've Found Gold!'" by Fergus M. Bordewich; *Reader's Digest*, February 1998
    Photograph on page 220 by Bettmann Archive/Getty Images; Illustration on page 222 by ullstein bild/Getty Images; Photographs on pages 223 and 225 by Gado/ Getty Images; Illustration on page 226 Courtesy of Library of Congress, LC-DIG-pga-08765; Photograph on page 227 by Fotosearch/Getty Images

"The Key Witness" by Lynn Rosellini; *Reader's Digest*, November 2007
    Photograph on page 234 photographed by Kelly Laduke

"The 39-Year-Old Apology" by Tom Hallman Jr., from the *Oregonian*; April 22, 2012, © 2012 by Oregonian Publishing Co.; *Reader's Digest*, October 2012
    Illustration on page 238 Illustrated by Shout; Photographs on page 241 left courtesy of James Atteberry; on page 241 right courtesy of Larry Israelson;

Where, Oh Where? Answers 36: C, Port Austin, Michigan (the lake in question is Lake Huron). **92: D,** Marfa, Texas (the hit TV show that the movie *Giant* inspired was *Dallas.* **146: A,** White Sands National Park, New Mexico. **182: C,** Gladewater, Texas. **246: B,** Iao Valley State Monument, Hawaii.

on page 242 photographed by Robbie McClaran

"Terror at the Beach" by Lisa Fitterman, Derek Burnett; *Reader's Digest*, August 2014
     Photographs on page 248 by wildestanimal/Getty Images; on page 255 top by AP Photo/ Michigan City Fire Department via The News Dispatch; on page 255 inset courtesy Woessner Family via The University of Chicago Hospital; on page 258 by Photographs by Miller Mobley

"—And Sudden Death" by J.C. Furnas; *Reader's Digest*, August 1935

"My Hut" by Cathrin Bradbury, from the *Toronto Star*; © 2022, Cathrin Bradbury, from "Why I Joined the Great Hut Rush of 2022," the *Toronto Star*, Jan. 22, 2022, *TheStar.com*; *Reader's Digest* international editions, October 2022
     Illustration on page 274 by Graham Roumieu

"Liar, Liar" by Andy Simmons; *Reader's Digest*, August 2011
     Illustrations on pages 280, 282, 283, 284 and 285 by Mark Matcho

Cartoon Credits
17 Mike Baldwin/CartoonStock; 65 Paul Kales; 81 Pat Byrnes; 119 Ian Baker/CartoonStock; 159 Susan Camilleri Konar; 194 Bob Mankoff/CartoonStock; 211 Thomas Bros; 231 Joseph Farris/CartoonStock; 263 Roy Delgado/CartoonStock; 279 Conan de Vries